Getting into

Law

Steven Boyes and Melanie Allen

11th edition

trotman

Getting into guides

Getting into Law

This 11th edition published in 2016 by Trotman Education, an imprint of Crimson Publishing Ltd, 19–21 Charles Street, Bath BA1 1HX.

Authors: Steven Boyes and Melanie Allen

© Trotman Publishing 2008, 2010, 2012, 2014, 2016

© Trotman & Co Ltd 1994, 1996, 1999, 2002, 2004, 2006

British Library Cataloguing in Publication Data
A catalogue record for this book is available from the British Library.

ISBN 978 1 911067 11 5

Typeset by IDSUK (DataConnection) Ltd
Printed and bound by TJ International Ltd, Padstow, Cornwall

Contents

Contents

Preface

Law has always been a sought after profession for students, and now, perhaps more than ever before, aspiring lawyers face tough competition at virtually every stage of their route to qualification, from securing a place on one of the 'best' university law degree courses to finding a job at the end of it all.

During the course of MPW's work advising students on their choice of university course and subsequent career path, we have gathered together a huge amount of information on law courses and the legal profession. With the encouragement of Trotman Publishing, that information has been brought together in this guide.

This edition has been substantially revised and updated. We hope that this guide will be useful to anyone considering a career in law.

MPW
November 2015

About the authors

Steven Boyes read Geography at Lancaster University and then undertook postgraduate research in employment law at Durham University, where he also completed a PGCE. He is Principal of MPW London and has been a director of the MPW Group since 1997.

Melanie Allen read Economics at King's College, Cambridge, before deciding to become a lawyer. She trained at Slaughter and May in London and qualified as a solicitor in 1993. Her varied legal career has encompassed working as a corporate lawyer in the City, an entertainment lawyer in the West End, and a wills and probate lawyer in a small high-street firm.

Acknowledgements

Many thanks are due to all those who have written previous editions of *Getting into Law*, and in particular to Lianne Carter.

We are also very grateful to the following people from BPP University Law Schools who have contributed to previous editions of this book: Peter Crisp, Mandy Gill, Jonathan Haines, Jill Livingstone, Carl Lygo, Rahim Shamji, Abigail Flack, Nicola Zoumidou and Neil Stewart.

Thanks are also due to other contributors to earlier editions of the book, in particular James Burnett, Fiona Hindle, James Holland, Julian Webb, Paul Whiteside, Mike Semple Piggot, Frances Burton, Joanne Hubert and Justina Burnett.

Finally, a special thank you to the young lawyers who have kindly taken the time to contribute the stories of their legal careers so far for the case studies: Karen, Elizabeth, Sarah, Peter, Paul, Claire, Katie Elly, Mark, Karen, Emma and Laura.

About this book

This book is written for anyone considering a career in law. Law is a perennial favourite as a career choice: it offers intellectual stimulation, ancient customs, a morally satisfying focus on justice and fairness, and potentially great financial rewards.

However, with popularity comes competition: now, more than ever before, competition for places to read law at university, solicitors' training contract places and barristers' pupillages is intense. You will therefore need to do your research and be as fully prepared as possible. We hope that this book will go some way towards arming you with the necessary information to help you to succeed.

The book will start with an introduction to the legal profession, an overview of the UK's legal systems, and a discussion of what lawyers do and how they fit into the legal systems.

The next two chapters will then outline how to qualify as a lawyer, including the different qualification routes, and then consider the importance of work experience.

The remaining chapters will guide you through the university application process, including choosing the right university law (or other) course, completing the UCAS form (including the all-important personal statement), preparing for an interview if necessary and what to do on results day. There is then a chapter outlining the arrangements for fees and funding for university degree courses.

At the end of the book there is a glossary of terms, relating to studying law, applying to university and qualifying as a lawyer.

Of course, you will still have to show lots of ability and drive to impress university law admissions tutors and your potential future employers. You should make sure that you:

- revise thoroughly for your exams and get the best grades you possibly can, giving you the widest choice of degree options.
- become a legal eagle and do your own research. Talk to your teachers, family, friends, lawyers and anyone else who knows something about the legal profession. Consider carefully what type of degree course is appropriate for you, or, indeed, whether you should even study law and become a lawyer in the first place. There is also a huge amount of information and guidance online, which the references in this book will help you find, so make sure that you use it!

1 | An introduction to the legal profession

Most people's first impressions of the legal profession come from the glamorous world of film and television. Legal dramas paint a picture of lawyers striding heroically across the courtroom of life, standing up for truth and justice. But what are lawyers and what do they actually do?

The term 'lawyer' is a loose one that covers barristers, solicitors, judges, legal executives, paralegals, in-house legal advisors, some civil servants and academic lawyers. In England and Wales, the crucial distinction to make is between the two main branches of the profession: solicitors and barristers. The legal professions in Scotland and Northern Ireland have a similar distinction and are outlined at the end of Chapter 3. The essential difference between solicitors and barristers relates to their respective rights to advocate on behalf of a client in court: traditionally only barristers were permitted to undertake advocacy on behalf of a client in the highest courts. This distinction means that law is sometimes referred to as a 'split' profession – but in fact the split is increasingly becoming blurred, due to modern reforms that permit solicitors to undertake further training and then represent clients in the higher courts. (The term 'attorney' is American and has no real meaning in the UK.)

Solicitors work on all aspects of the law, but do not normally present their clients' cases in court.

Barristers are instructed by solicitors to represent their clients in the courtroom or give opinions on specific points of law.

The main focus of this book is on the solicitors' and barristers' professions, but there are many other careers within the legal field that can also be pursued, and also many non-legal careers for which a law degree might provide a good foundation. More information on this is given in the paragraphs below.

Solicitors

Solicitors are often described as being like medical general practitioners (GPs). They deal directly with their clients and often have an ongoing professional and/or business relationship with them. Solicitors in private practice group together in law firm partnerships, with the senior solicitors being partners and the more junior solicitors being employed assistants. Most solicitors now deal with specific areas of the law, for example employment or family law or, in the City, specialist areas such as syndicated loans, bonds or takeovers and mergers. In this respect they differ from GPs, who are usually generalists.

However, in most cases, law firms cover a wide area of legal practice; this means that in smaller firms solicitors may be required to cover a broader range of areas, whereas the larger law firms will have specialists in very narrow areas of law.

Historically, solicitors could only appear in lower courts, such as the magistrates' and county courts. These days, however, solicitors who obtain higher rights of audience can appear in the higher courts, including the Supreme Court, and may even apply to become QCs (Queen's Counsel), although this is still rare.

The Law Society is the body that represents and supports solicitors in England and Wales. The Solicitors Regulation Authority is the independent regulator of solicitors and law firms in England and Wales, and deals with all regulatory and disciplinary matters, including:

- setting the standards for qualifying as a solicitor
- administering the roll (register) of solicitors
- drafting the rules of professional conduct
- monitoring solicitors and their firms to make sure that they are complying with the rules.

Barristers

Barristers have traditionally been described as more like medical consultants. They are 'self-employed referral professionals' who are often, although not exclusively, trial lawyers – meaning that they appear robed and wigged in court on behalf of their clients. Clients are usually referred to them by a professional advisor, often a solicitor – although modern reforms allow barristers to see the public directly where the Bar Council has agreed that no referral is necessary (for example in relation to tax advice when referred by an accountant).

It is usual for barristers (often called counsel) to specialise in certain areas of law, for example criminal law, company law or tax law and so on. Barristers in private practice group together in chambers, sharing overheads and office support, but remaining self-employed professionals.

Barristers in England and Wales are represented by the Bar Council, which promotes barristers' services and upholds ethical standards in the profession. The Bar Standards Board performs a similar function to the Solicitors Regulation Authority, and is responsible for regulating barristers in the public interest. Its functions include:

- setting the education and training requirements for becoming a barrister
- setting the standards of conduct for barristers
- monitoring the service provided by barristers.

Legal executives

Legal executives are lawyers who have not undertaken the professional training required to become a solicitor or barrister, but have qualified instead with the Chartered Institute of Legal Executives (CILEX). Historically, the modern legal executive role evolved from the role of law clerks, who used to help solicitors with their cases. In the 1960s, the legal executives' profession was created in order to offer a recognised career path.

The Legal Services Act 2007 made chartered legal executives 'authorised persons' who are able to undertake 'reserved legal activities' alongside solicitors and barristers. Qualified chartered legal executives can now do much of the same work that solicitors do, but are trained to work in one or two areas of the law rather than having a broader, more general, legal training like solicitors. They can become partners in law firms and even judges.

Legal executives are regulated by CILEX, which offers various routes into qualifying as a legal executive. It is possible to become a qualified legal executive without having obtained a degree. There is also a graduate fast-track diploma for those who have obtained a law degree or Graduate Diploma in Law (see 'Do I need a law degree?' below). The Institute offers an accessible and cost-effective route to becoming a lawyer. Further information is available at www.cilex.org.uk.

Other lawyers

The Legal Services Act 2007 also defined various other groups of lawyers as being entitled to undertake reserved legal activities. These lawyers are trained and qualified in particular specialist areas of law and often work in law firms alongside solicitors. They are notaries, licensed conveyancers, law costs draftsmen, trademark agents and patent agents. Further information can be found at www.thenotariessociety.org.uk (for notaries), www.clc-uk.org (for licensed conveyancers), www.associationofcostslawyers.co.uk (for law costs draftsmen), www.itma.org.uk (trademark agents) and www.cipa.org.uk (for patent agents).

Size and make-up of the legal profession (England and Wales)

Solicitors

The solicitors' profession in England and Wales is the largest branch of the legal profession. In 2014 its governing body, the Law Society (www.lawsociety.org.uk), reported that there were 160,394 registered solicitors and 130,382 of these held a practising certificate. To qualify as a solicitor you would normally be expected to complete a training contract period of employment that lasts two years. In the year to July 2014 the Law Society reported that 5,001 trainee solicitors commenced training contracts.

The solicitors' profession is divided between solicitors who work in private practice for law firms and those who work 'in-house' (i.e. for companies, government legal departments and so on). In 2014 there were 9,542 private law firms employing 90,306 solicitors, meaning that 56% of all solicitors on the roll were working in private practice. The number of solicitors employed outside private practice amounted to 25,325. In 2014, almost 40% of practising solicitors were located in London, with almost half of these (nearly 20% of the total) in City firms.

Of all the practising solicitors in 2014, 48% were women, although women now make up the majority of admissions to the roll (i.e. newly qualified solicitors) at around 60%. The proportion of practising solicitors who are from minority ethnic groups continues to grow and was 15% in 2014.

Barristers

The barristers' profession, known as the Bar, is much smaller than the solicitors' profession. According to the Bar Standards Board (www.barstandardsboard.org.uk), in December 2014 there were a total of 15,716 barristers in practice, of whom 35% were women and 11.5% described themselves as belonging to an ethnic minority. Most practising barristers (12,709 in 2014) are self-employed. A further 2,794 barristers are in employed practice.

	Number	% women (approx)	% in London (approx)
Solicitors	130,382	48%	40%
– private practice	– 90,306		
– in-house	– 25,325		
Barristers	15,716	35%	66%
– self-employed	– 12,709		
– employed	– 2,794		

Table 1: Solicitors and barristers in practice (England and Wales) in 2014

Legal executives and other lawyers

The much younger legal executives' profession is smaller still: the Chartered Institute of Legal Executives (www.cilex.org.uk) reported in 2015 that there were around 7,500 qualified chartered legal executives, of whom 250 were partners in law firms. The total number of members of the Institute (including paralegals and other legal professionals) was around 20,000, of whom 74% were women. More than a third of their new members are of an ethnic minority.

The other groups of lawyers mentioned above (notaries, licensed conveyancers, law costs draftsmen, trademark agents and patent agents) are also much smaller in number than solicitors or barristers. This book will therefore focus on the two main branches of the legal profession: solicitors and barristers.

Gender balance

It is difficult to imagine that less than 100 years ago the legal profession was the preserve of men. Things have changed and are still changing. The Law Society reports that just over 60% of training contracts are now issued to women. About 48% of practising solicitors are female, and, in July 2014, there were nearly 8,000 women partners in law firms. Around 60% of practising solicitors under the age of 35 are now women. The Law Society's most recent report suggests that, based on the rates of growth recorded over the past five years, the number of women practising solicitors will equal the number of men by 2017. There has been a feeling within the solicitors' profession in the past that not enough female solicitors make it to partnership in some of the very large law firms, and there is still a substantial difference between the representation of men and women at partner level. However, the gap has been narrowing over recent years. The percentage of women solicitors working outside private practice, i.e. in-house, is higher.

About 35% of practising barristers are women, with 44% of new entrants undertaking pupillage being female. Whereas in the past it was difficult for women to break down the traditional barriers, today the profession is increasingly open to all. This is evident in the fact that in 2013–14 just under 50% of barristers called to the Bar were women.

However, there is still progress to be made by women in terms of judicial appointments. Just over a quarter of all judges in England and Wales are women, only eight out of 38 Appeal Court judges are women, and only one woman has made it to the most senior judicial appointment (a Supreme Court judge). Efforts are being made to increase the number of female judges and the number is increasing every year. It will, however, take time before parity can be reached.

The majority (74%) of members of the Chartered Institute of Legal Executives are women.

Chapter 3 contains more details about the legal profession, where lawyers work, and what they do. Chapter 4 contains details about how to qualify as a lawyer.

Do I need a law degree?

The legal profession in England and Wales is virtually unique in not requiring all entrants to have a law degree. In fact, many non-law graduates enter the profession through the full-time Graduate Diploma in Law programme (an intensive one-year postgraduate course for non-law graduates covering the essential foundation subjects taught as part of a law degree). The Law Society reported in 2014 that non-law graduates made up almost 40% of direct entrants to the solicitors' profession (i.e. graduates who go straight into the solicitors' profession). A substantial percentage of entrants to the barristers' profession is also non-law graduates. The skills acquired on many non-law degrees are often highly sought after by legal recruiters. For example, language skills or scientific/technical skills may be particularly useful in certain areas of law, and humanities degrees teach and test many of the skills that are essential for a lawyer, such as the ability to research information and analyse and present it in a clear and concise way. It is therefore important to bear in mind that you do not need a law degree to become a lawyer and many employers positively welcome applications from non-law graduates who can offer broader skills in other areas. There are, however, cost implications due to the extra year of postgraduate study that will be required (see Chapter 4, page 43 for more details).

It is also important to be aware that not every law degree is recognised by the professional bodies as a qualifying law degree (QLD) that will satisfy the requirements for the academic stage of training. It depends on the subjects that are studied on the course. This means that, if you do decide to do a law degree, you must be careful when choosing your course. The Solicitors Regulation Authority (SRA) and the Bar Standards Board (BSB) keep registers of which degrees are approved QLDs and these are available on their respective websites. See Chapter 6 for further details.

Similarly, many students graduate with degrees in law and then, for whatever reason, do not go on to qualify as a solicitor or barrister. The number of law graduates compared with the number of professional training places available is very telling: according to the Law Society, 16,116 students graduated with law degrees from universities in England and Wales in 2013–14. This number continues to rise each year: it was 11,139 in 2004 and 13,433 in 2009. The number of law graduates in England and Wales in 2014 was therefore 45% higher than in 2004. These figures only include those with 'straight' law degrees and not those with joint honours degrees that include law, so the total number of law graduates is likely to be considerably higher.

However, the limited number of training places available means that many undergraduate law students do not carry on to qualify as solicitors or barristers. The number of solicitors' training contracts registered annually has, according to the Law Society, remained stable at around 5,000 since 2009–10. For aspiring barristers, in 2013/14, only 397 obtained their first six months' pupillage (the first part of the mandatory 12-month training stage for those who want to practise as a barrister). Some law graduates will also enter the legal profession via the graduate fast-track diploma to become legal executives, but there are still considerably more law graduates than entrants to the legal professions. Therefore, the link between taking a law degree and becoming a qualified lawyer is not nearly as clear cut as many people believe, and one definitely does not imply the other.

What if I don't want to go into the law after my degree?

As well as those who, unfortunately, do not manage to get into one of the legal professions after taking a law degree, there are also some students who study law with no intention of becoming a professional lawyer. The legal knowledge and additional skills gained from a law degree are highly prized and can be applied to a number of jobs.

But what else can a law graduate do other than law? Many public figures have degrees in law that have led them in all sorts of different directions, from politicians to comedians. Other careers that a law degree can lead to are:

- **Accountancy.** Many aspects of accountancy relate to those found in legal practice, such as analysing large amounts of technical material, writing reports and advising clients. Law graduates are often particularly attracted by tax consultancy.
- **Civil service.** If you are interested in policy making and implementation, then you might think about a career in the civil service. Administrators such as civil servants need a methodical and precise approach, as well as good writting and communication skills – all skills that are developed and honed on a law degree course. Some government departments, such as the Home Office, HM Revenue & Customs, the Ministry of Justice and the Foreign & Commonwealth Office, have particular legal responsibilities and might be especially attractive to law graduates. Local government and the health service are also possibilities for public sector careers in administration.

- **Commerce and industry**. The skills you learn from a law degree will also be invaluable in the world of commerce and industry, where there are career opportunities in general business management.
- **Banking and finance**. A number of law graduates are lured into the highly paid world of banking and finance, where a legal background can certainly be useful.

Law graduates also go into many other areas, such as legal publishing, the media, journalism (legal or otherwise), the police service, teaching, human resources and more.

Some law graduates choose not to pursue the training to become either a solicitor or a barrister, or, indeed a legal executive, but would still like to do something in the legal field. They will often move into areas such as paralegal or clerking work. Paralegals research cases, scan and collate documents and generally assist qualified lawyers in their work. Clerks undertake duties such as taking witness statements on behalf of solicitors' clients and conducting legal research for solicitors, barristers and others plus any administrative work that is required.

Case study

Karen did not consider a legal career until speaking to a careers advisor after her A level exams. She chose to study for a law degree hoping it would open doors to whichever career she decided to pursue. Over the course of the degree she was fascinated by law as a subject and its relevance to everyday life. After her degree Karen decided to gain some commercial experience in the legal sector. She began training as a law costs draftsman; someone who deals with cases after they have concluded and draws up bills of the work done in order for the solicitor to be paid. The role of a law costs draftsman includes negotiating costs when they are disputed by paying parties, and attending hearings as an advocate to argue these costs. Karen enjoys the fact that legal costs is a fast-moving, exciting area of law, and believes that a career as a costs draftsman would be ideal for someone who is mathematically minded, yet also enjoys advocacy. Karen is now a director of her own very successful law costing business.

Therefore, not only do you not need a law degree to become a lawyer, but you also do not need to become a lawyer just because you have a law degree. This book is written for anyone with an interest in the law – either as a degree, or as a career, or both.

2 | The UK's legal systems

This chapter looks predominantly at the English legal system; however, the Scottish and Northern Irish legal systems are outlined at the end of the chapter. Welsh law mainly follows that of England, but there are a few important differences, such as the Welsh Language Act 1993, which puts the Welsh language on an equal footing with English in the conduct of public business and the administration of justice in Wales. See www.assemblywales.org for more information.

The English legal system

English law comes from two main sources: statute law made by Parliament (also known as 'Acts of Parliament' or 'legislation') and case law made by judges (also known as 'common law'). The UK's membership of the European Union and the Human Rights Act 1998 have also significantly impacted on the English legal system. These sources will be summarised below, together with a brief description of the court structure.

Statute law

Parliament is the supreme law-making body in the English legal system, and is made up of the House of Commons, the House of Lords, and the Monarch. The House of Commons is made up of democratically elected Members of Parliament (MPs) from various political parties, and it is the political party that has the majority of MPs elected to the House of Commons that will form a government. (Note: in the 2010 election no political party gained a majority, which is why a coalition government was formed.)

The House of Lords is made up of the most senior bishops in the Church of England and life peers who are nominated by the Prime Minister and then appointed by the Monarch. There are also a few hereditary peers. Since the 1990s, there have been calls for reform of the House of Lords, including the suggestion that a proportion of the members be democratically elected. In May 2011 the government published detailed proposals for reform of the House of Lords, but the plans were dropped in August 2012. Instead, the House of Lords Reform Act 2014 introduced much more minor reforms, including allowing Lords to retire or be disqualified for non-attendance.

New laws are mostly put forward by the government, and the draft legislation has to go through several stages of debates and votes in both the House of Commons and the House of Lords. In the vast majority of cases, the draft legislation has to be approved by both houses in order for it to become law. The final stage in the legislative process is Royal Assent, which is where the Monarch gives approval to the draft legislation and at this point it becomes an Act of Parliament. This is merely a formality and the last time that a monarch refused assent was in 1707.

Acts of Parliament cannot be challenged by the courts, and can only be changed by a subsequent piece of legislation. Acts of Parliament are also known as 'primary legislation' because they are made by Parliament, the supreme law-making body. Parliament can delegate its law-making power to other bodies, including government departments and local authorities, and law made by such bodies is known as delegated legislation or secondary legislation. Delegated legislation is subject to the control of Parliament and can be challenged in the courts.

Common law

Although Parliament is the supreme law-making body, and judges are simply supposed to apply the laws made by Parliament in cases, the doctrine of judicial precedent and the rules of statutory interpretation mean that in practice judges also make law through decided cases. This is known as 'case law' or 'common law' and is a major source of law in the English legal system.

The doctrine of judicial precedent is based on the Latin maxim 'stare decisis' which means 'stand by what has been decided', so, very simply, when a judge makes a decision in a case, this should be followed in future cases that are similar. The system of precedent operates through the court hierarchy, so that only certain (higher) courts create binding precedents (precedents that must be followed in future cases). Precedents are created when a new situation or point of law comes up in a case that is not provided for in legislation and has not been decided in a previous case, so the judge has to decide the case by looking at situations that are similar and use reasoning by analogy.

When judges are applying legislation to cases before them, it is not always possible to simply take the words of the statute and decide the case, because words can have more than one meaning. In addition, new technology and changes in society can mean that it is not clear whether the legislation applies in some cases. This is where the rules of statutory interpretation come in. Some judges take a 'literal approach' of applying the ordinary meaning of the words in the legislation even if this leads to an absurd result, whereas other judges take a 'purposive approach' and decide the case based on what they think Parliament wanted to achieve through the legislation. When a judge makes an interpretation in a case, this can create a precedent so that future cases must follow this interpretation.

Common law as a source of law only works because of the system of law reporting in England and Wales; an accurate record of decided cases is kept so that it can be referred to by judges and lawyers in future cases. It is mostly decisions of the higher courts in the English legal system that are reported, and all High Court, Court of Appeal and Supreme Court cases are now available on the internet, for example from the British and Irish Legal Information Institute (www.bailii.org).

European Union law

In 1973 the UK joined the European Economic Community (EEC), which was established in 1957 by Germany, France, Italy, Belgium, the Netherlands and Luxembourg. In 1993 the EEC became the European Union (EU). Over the years European law has had an increasing impact on the legal systems of Member States. There are now 28 Member States.

The European Union produces its own primary and secondary legislation, and has its own court, the European Court of Justice. Case law has confirmed that European law is supreme over the national laws of Member States, and that national law must be interpreted in accordance with European law.

Human Rights Act 1998

The Human Rights Act 1998 officially incorporated the European Convention on Human Rights into the English legal system. The Convention sets out certain fundamental rights of the citizens of Europe, including the right to life, the right to a fair trial and the right to respect for private and family life. Prior to the Human Rights Act 1998, English citizens who believed that their human rights had been infringed had to take their case to the European Court of Human Rights in Strasbourg. The Human Rights Act 1998 means that such cases can now be dealt with in the courts of the English legal system.

The Human Rights Act 1998 has affected the English legal system in several other ways, including obligations that our courts must take into account any decision of the European Court of Human Rights, and, so far as is possible to do so, interpret national legislation so that it is compatible with the European Convention on Human Rights. All draft legislation must also state whether or not it is compatible with the Convention. This is intended to encourage the government and civil service to consider the human rights implications of proposed legislation before it is introduced.

Court structure

The court structure in England is divided into two systems: those courts with civil jurisdiction and those with criminal jurisdiction. Civil cases are private disputes between individuals or companies. There are many different types of civil law, including family law, employment law, the law of contract, the law of tort and commercial law. Criminal cases are where the state prosecutes people for breaking laws, even though there is usually a victim.

Most civil cases are heard, in the first instance, by the county courts, but in cases where large amounts of money are in dispute, they will initially be heard in the High Court. Appeals from both the county courts and the High Court can be made up through the court hierarchy.

All minor criminal matters are dealt with by the magistrates' court. Serious cases are referred to the crown court. Here, the case will be decided upon by a lay jury, a fundamental part of the criminal justice system. Cases can be appealed from the magistrates' court to the crown court and from there to the Court of Appeal (Criminal Division).

The highest court in the land is now the UK Supreme Court, which is the final court of appeal for civil cases throughout the UK, and for criminal cases from England, Wales and Northern Ireland. The Supreme Court replaced the Appellate Committee of the House of Lords in 2009. It only considers appeals that concern points of law of general public or constitutional importance. Each case is normally heard by five Justices of the Supreme Court. When a court is considering a point of European law it may refer to the European Court of Justice in Luxembourg for interpretation. The Judicial Committee of the Privy Council is the court of final appeal for many current and former Commonwealth countries, UK overseas territories and Crown dependencies. In the year ending 31 March 2014, the Privy Council heard 51 appeals. By far the most contentious work relates to appeals against the death penalty.

Judges

In contrast with many other European countries, the judiciary in England and Wales is not a separate career. Judges are appointed from both main branches of the legal profession. Chartered legal executives can also now become judges.

Judges in the Supreme Court are known as Justices of the Supreme Court (formerly Law Lords in the House of Lords) and judges in the Court of Appeal are known as Lord or Lady Justices of Appeal. In the

High Court, there are High Court judges and also masters and registrars, who hear certain types of applications.

Circuit judges, recorders and district judges are the remaining three types of judges. Circuit judges sit either in the crown court (to try criminal cases) or in the county courts (to hear civil cases). Recorders are part-time circuit judges, and district judges sit in the magistrates' courts and county courts.

Alternatively, a panel of lay magistrates can try criminal cases in the magistrates' court. They are not legally qualified or paid but are respected members of the community who sit as magistrates on a part-time basis.

New members of the judiciary are selected by the Judicial Appointments Commission, an independent body that was created specifically for this purpose following the Constitutional Reform Act 2005. The aim was to provide a fair and transparent selection process. Once appointed, judges are completely independent of both the legislature and the executive, and so are free to administer justice without fear of political interference. Justices of the Supreme Court are not selected by the Judicial Appointments Commission, but are instead selected by a special Supreme Court Selection Commission.

Tribunals

A system of tribunals operates alongside the court system. Each type of tribunal specialises in a particular area of law. For example, Employment Tribunals handle workplace disputes between employers and employees. These include disputed deductions from wages, unfair dismissal, redundancy and discrimination. A tribunal is a more informal setting than a court. There are no judges; tribunals are chaired by a legally qualified tribunal judge, who will often sit with specialist non-legal members who have particular experience in the subject matter of the tribunal. In Employment Tribunals, for example, a chairman will be assisted by two lay members. There is no standard form of procedure. Nonetheless, they operate in a similar way to court proceedings, with witnesses usually giving evidence on oath.

Reform

The English legal system is constantly changing, so it is very important you keep up to date with current affairs in the legal field if you are thinking about a legal career. Essential preparation for a legal career includes reading a good quality (i.e. broadsheet) newspaper such as The Times. You can also look at professional journals such as The Law Society Gazette and The Lawyer, which are both available online. Further details and website addresses are contained in Chapter 12.

The Scottish legal system

Scotland has its own legal system, with significant differences from those of the other constituent nations of the United Kingdom. The two fundamental differences are the role of the Scottish Parliament in formulating legislation, and the basis of Scottish jurisprudence in a mixed system of uncodified civil law and common law.

Since 1999, the Scottish Parliament has been responsible for legislating on a wide range of domestic matters relating to Scotland, but there are certain policy areas reserved for the UK Parliament at Westminster. Notably, these include constitutional matters, defence and national security policy, foreign policy, and fiscal and economic policy. Scotland's legal system and court structure is separate and autonomous from that of England and Wales and Northern Ireland. Historically, it has its basis in Roman law, with some English common law influence since the Act of Union of 1707. Recent developments in Scottish law have seen the strong influence of English (and other jurisdictions') common law, as well as the influence and incorporation of European Union law.

While some areas of law are similar to that of England, Scotland has its own system of criminal law and procedure, of civil procedure, and of certain areas of private law (such as land law). The court system reflects these differences, with its own system of separate criminal and civil courts. By way of illustration, the Court of Session is Scotland's supreme court for civil cases and the High Court of Justiciary is Scotland's supreme court for criminal cases. Decisions of the High Court of Justiciary are not generally subject to review by the UK Supreme Court, which reflects Scotland's distinctive tradition of criminal law and procedure. Most cases in Scotland are dealt with in either the Sheriff Court, which deals with the majority of civil cases and more serious criminal offences, or the Justice of the Peace Court, which deals with less serious criminal offences. Tribunals also sit in Scotland. The legal profession in Scotland is outlined in Chapter 3.

> For more information see
>
> www.scotcourts.gov.uk/about-the-scottish-court-service.

The Northern Irish legal system

Like Scotland, Northern Ireland (NI) has a legal system separate from that of England and Wales. Unlike Scotland, NI's legal system to a large extent mirrors that of England and Wales, with the following differences.

In terms of legislative law, the Northern Ireland Assembly (which gained legislative powers in 1999 following the Good Friday Agreement) has the power to make laws for NI on all transferred matters, which are generally in the economic and social field. The Westminster Parliament retains responsibility for matters of national importance, such as the constitution, national security, defence and foreign policy. The Assembly operates under a unique power-sharing arrangement between the two main political communities in Northern Ireland.

NI has its own judicial system (the Northern Ireland Courts and Tribunals Service), which parallels that of England and Wales. It includes the Court of Appeal, the High Court of Justice in Northern Ireland, the crown court, magistrates' courts and county courts. The highest court of appeal for both criminal and civil matters, as in England and Wales, is the UK Supreme Court. Judicial law in NI partially derives from English common law and is based on the doctrine of judicial precedent. It has developed along very similar lines to that of English common law. English precedent from the higher courts is not, however, binding, but is deemed to be persuasive. The higher Northern Irish courts also pay attention to important decisions made in the Republic of Ireland (ROI), the major Commonwealth nations and even the USA. The legal profession in Northern Ireland will be outlined in Chapter 3.

> For more information please see www.niassembly.gov.uk, www.gov.uk/guidance/devolution-settlement-northern-ireland and www.nidirect.gov.uk/index/information-and-services/crime-justice-and-the-law.

3| What do lawyers do?

The legal profession in England and Wales is divided into two main branches: solicitors and barristers, as explained in Chapter 1. This chapter will run through the working practices of each of the branches of the profession in more detail. At the end of the chapter there is an overview of the legal profession in Scotland and Northern Ireland.

Solicitors

Solicitors' work is as diverse as life itself – they will be behind the scenes offering legal advice to their clients on everything from corporate takeovers to individual personal injury claims. The working life varies enormously depending on where solicitors work. As mentioned in Chapter 1, about 56% of all practising solicitors work in private practice for law firms: the rest work in-house either for companies or for government agencies, etc. Even for those working in law firms, the work will be completely different depending on the type of firm. For example, in a large firm it is not unusual to be working as part of a team of lawyers on one large case for several months, whereas in a small firm you may have 20 or more cases on the go at one time and be solely responsible for dealing with these.

This section offers a brief overview of the different types of law firms and the sort of work that the solicitors who work in them undertake.

Large corporate firms

The largest law firms by turnover tend to be the big corporate law firms specialising in corporate and finance law, which usually have their headquarters in the City of London. Most of them also have large international operations. Data on these firms is collected and published regularly by the legal press and shows turnover, number of lawyers employed, profits per partner, etc.

There are broad categories into which these law firms are placed. There is a certain amount of debate about which firms should be in which category, and the precise picture changes annually, as some firms will grow faster than others, and the profitability of each firm will clearly vary year on year. There are also fairly frequent mergers between law firms. Therefore, all the categories in this chapter are broadbrush generalisations, and the lists of law firms within them should be viewed as illustrative examples only.

The Lawyer newspaper (which is available online) publishes a report in October every year on the top 200 law firms. The Legal 500 also publishes a directory of law firm profiles and this is also available online (www.legal500.com/books/l500/directory). The general picture at the time of writing is as follows:

Magic Circle

There is a 'Magic Circle' of the most prestigious large international corporate firms which are based in London. The generally accepted view at the moment is that the Magic Circle firms are:

- Allen & Overy (992 UK lawyers)
- Clifford Chance (969 UK lawyers)
- Freshfields Bruckhaus Deringer
- Linklaters (1,100 UK lawyers)
- Slaughter and May (721 UK lawyers).

The figures in brackets are the number of UK fee earners in each firm (comprising partners, assistants, trainees and legal executives) and are taken from The Legal 500 at the date of writing where available.

These firms can offer great rewards, with high salaries and high profits per partner. However, the work often involves working long hours in a high-pressure environment. The first four firms have an extensive network of international offices, whereas Slaughter and May instead has strong links with selected overseas firms for international work. In general, many major London law firms have expanded considerably internationally.

Silver Circle

The term 'Silver Circle' of law firms is an informal term, coined by *The Lawyer* in 2005, to refer to those elite firms that are ranked just below the Magic Circle in terms of turnover, but still have considerably higher profits per partner than other firms, together with a premium client base. These firms are also based in London, but most also have an international network of overseas offices.

The Silver Circle is a less settled group than the Magic Circle, but, at the time of writing, the firms within it are generally considered to be:

- Ashurst (2,220 UK lawyers)
- Berwin Leighton Paisner
- Herbert Smith Freehills (861 UK lawyers)
- SJ Berwin (now part of King & Wood Mallesons following a 2013 merger)
- Macfarlanes (341 UK lawyers)
- Travers Smith (327 UK lawyers).

There are significant differences between these Silver Circle firms, for example in terms of total revenue (although they are all in the top 50 for total revenue). The size and the number of international offices for each firm differ considerably.

American firms

The trend for large leading US law firms to open branches in London has continued apace and the largest US firms are now firmly entrenched in the UK legal market.

The US law firms with significant London branches include:

- Latham & Watkins (250 UK lawyers)
- White & Case (310 UK lawyers)
- Kirkland & Ellis (152 UK lawyers)
- Skadden, Arps, Slate, Meagher & Flom
- Weil, Gotshal & Manges (160 UK lawyers)
- Shearman & Sterling (180 UK lawyers).

Other major City firms

In addition to the Magic Circle and Silver Circle, some other large, well-respected City firms are:

- Clyde & Co.
- CMS (817 UK lawyers)
- Dentons (371 UK lawyers)
- Hogan Lovells (620+ UK lawyers)
- Norton Rose Fulbright (670+ UK lawyers).

Major national and regional firms

If London is not for you, then there are some very large national and regional law firms with a major presence in large cities outside London. They offer the chance to do top-quality work with high-profile clients outside London. Some of these firms have branches all over the country and many also have offices abroad, or have associate offices abroad. These major national and regional law firms include:

- DAC Beachcroft (1,444 UK lawyers)
- DLA Piper (1,263 UK lawyers).
- Eversheds
- Irwin Mitchell (1,100+ UK lawyers)
- Pinsent Masons (1,680+ UK lawyers).

What is the work like?

Large law firms tend to offer a comprehensive service to corporate clients, covering areas such as:

- company law
- mergers and acquisitions
- banking/finance law
- capital markets

- commercial litigation
- commercial property law
- competition law
- employment and pensions law
- financial regulatory law
- intellectual property law (i.e. copyright, trademarks and patents).

Work is often undertaken by teams, and the most junior members of the team may have little or no direct contact with the client. A typical area of work for a trainee involves conducting practical legal research or undertaking document checking work known as 'due diligence'.

Large corporate law firms tend to demand extremely high standards from their lawyers, who are well known for working long hours. In exchange, however, these firms offer excellent training and high salaries. They also usually offer good benefits, such as gym memberships, and also in-house catering services, possibly to avoid you ever having to leave your desk!

Most of the larger law firms will sponsor students that they have given training contracts to by paying their course fees for the Legal Practice Course and Graduate Diploma in Law (the postgraduate qualifications necessary to become a solicitor – see Chapter 4 for more details). In most cases, they also offer a maintenance grant. For more information on the sponsorship and maintenance grants offered by solicitors' firms, visit https://targetjobs.co.uk/career-sectors/law-solicitors.

Starting salaries for trainees in City firms tend to be high, with typical training contract salaries for major law firms in London about £35–£45,000 per annum and many firms offering at least £55,000 upon qualification, with some paying up to £80,000. However, for smaller firms outside of London the figures are not as high (see below).

Usually the larger law firms recruit two to three years ahead of when they expect the trainee to start work, and most will have a vacation placement scheme which typically takes place twice yearly, during the Easter and summer periods. As you can imagine, the large law firms tend to be massively over-subscribed. It is not unusual for a lawyer to leave a large law firm once qualified and move to a smaller firm for what is regarded as a better quality of life (i.e. shorter working hours).

Case study

Elizabeth initially won a place at the University of Cambridge to study veterinary medicine after taking A levels in biology, chemistry, physics, Latin and French. However, she quickly realised that she was not enjoying veterinary medicine at all.

'Many of my friends were law students and I had overheard their conversations with great interest; as soon as I got back to Cambridge after my first year, I started to devour law textbooks and finally approached the Law Director of Studies and asked if she would take me on. The central reason behind my choice was interest. Law is more language-based and contains aspects of history, politics, the English language and some philosophy and science, and makes use of writing, problem solving and debating skills.

'I chose to become a solicitor rather than a barrister because certain aspects of the profession – teamwork, more job stability, having a more stable and developed relationship with the client – appealed to me over the corresponding features of the Bar. The career path for solicitors, which allows you to have a job offer by the beginning of your final year of undergraduate study, was also an advantage.'

While at university, Elizabeth did three vacation schemes with large City solicitors' firms and also attended an open day at a fourth. 'I only applied for training contracts with firms I had done a vacation scheme with, as I had had the opportunity to gain a sense of the atmosphere and culture of the office.

'I received offers of training contracts from two of these firms and would have been happy to work for either. However, I chose my current firm (a major corporate US firm) because of the small trainee intake, the entrepreneurial system of picking up work (which I didn't think would suit me at all, but was pleasantly surprised by on the vacation scheme) and most importantly the open, friendly and non-hierarchical culture of the office.'

Elizabeth's first seat for her training contract is in the Regulatory department. 'It is turning out to be a great first seat. I work for around ten or eleven hours a day steadily, and get work from every Regulatory lawyer. In quiet moments I have also picked up some corporate work and some pro bono work. I have only been in the job a few weeks, so I haven't had direct client contact yet, but I have had contact with the firm's lawyers in other offices and with the Financial Conduct Authority. I have been doing a mixture of routine trainee tasks (proofreading, copying and collating documents, telephone notes) with some more exciting research work as well.'

So far, Elizabeth considers the key qualities needed for her job to be: 'attention to detail, enthusiasm, tenacity, the ability to deal with time pressure, organisation and self-motivation.'

Case study

After completing her law degree at Sussex University, Sarah took the Legal Practice Course at the University of Law. She then began her training contract at a large regional firm, having first undertaken a vacation scheme at the firm in her second year of university.

'The vacation scheme was a great opportunity to see what the firm was really like and to get involved in the type of work carried out by the trainees.'

Since qualifying as a solicitor in the firm's corporate team, Sarah's work has mainly focused on mergers and acquisitions, and she has been involved in sales and purchases of businesses ranging from £100,000 to £80 million in value.

'I have enjoyed being part of a relatively small team which has allowed me to work closely with our partners, have hands-on experience with clients and be fully involved in the deals. My responsibility on these transactions has grown over the past two years, and I now supervise the trainees and paralegals in our team. From my experience, in terms of obtaining a training contract, becoming a paralegal first can be a huge advantage – it is effectively a year-long interview, where if someone becomes a key part of a team and really gets stuck in, it can be hard not to want to offer them a training contract.'

Smaller law firms

These make up the largest number of law firms, and range in size from one solicitor (sole practitioner) to firms with over 50 lawyers. They tend to specialise in areas more relevant to individuals than companies, or have smaller company clients. For example, on most high streets or in smaller town centres you will find at least one small firm dealing with:

- civil litigation (disputes between individuals)
- conveyancing (sale and purchase of property)
- wills, probate and trusts
- employment law
- family law
- criminal law.

Due to the location of their offices, these firms tend to be categorised as high-street firms – but remember that small firms can still offer high-quality corporate work if they have the clients, and every high street is surrounded by small businesses! Do not forget that most large cities will have many small commercial firms dealing with good commercial work, as well as true high-street firms which concentrate more on individuals. Larger firms may take half a dozen trainees a year, whereas the smallest firms may recruit trainees only occasionally as the need arises.

Typically a trainee solicitor in a small firm will have much more client contact from an early stage. You may still be working as part of a team, but normally you will work closely with the supervisor and, upon qualification, you will work autonomously. It is not unusual to have a high degree of responsibility, and even partnership, cast upon you early on.

The financial rewards might not be as high as those in the larger law firms – but smaller law firms tend to offer a different quality of life (i.e. shorter hours) and work that is more related to everyday life. The SRA's minimum required salary for trainees was scrapped in 2014 although employers must pay at least the national minimum wage. Typical trainee starting salaries are around £25,000 in London and £20,000 outside London. Usually small firms do not offer any support with course fees or maintenance. Once qualified, starting salaries (although they vary depending on the type of firm and its locality) tend to be in the approximate region of £30,000, depending on the area of qualification.

Case study

Peter studied English literature, French and history at A level, after initially considering careers in both journalism and law. 'I decided to study history at the University of Southampton, as that was the subject that I enjoyed the most and I graduated with a 2.i.

'I became more interested in law by speaking to students who were actually studying law, and when I was called to do jury service one summer. Having assessed my strengths and weaknesses, I felt I had the correct skills to become a solicitor.' Peter then took the Graduate Diploma in Law after completing his degree.

'Although I was interested from an academic perspective in being a barrister, I felt I did not have the correct grades to be considered. I also felt that I would enjoy the role of a solicitor more. For example, I really liked the idea of having regular contact with lay people, working in a large team and undertaking non-contentious work.'

Peter made sure that he obtained some work experience while at university: 'I spent two summers working at a small firm in Chancery Lane, where I gained experience in commercial and civil litigation. I also did work experience at a regional firm in Dorset, where I did some more commercial work, and I did work placements at two global firms, where I gained experience in intel-lectual property and employment. I then did work experience at a high-street firm in West London where I assisted in the convey-ancing department.'

Peter is now a conveyancing solicitor at a large, multi-office high-street firm, having started working at the firm as a paralegal. 'When I was interviewed for a paralegal position, I learnt that the firm recruits each paralegal for a year to assess if they have what it takes to be a successful solicitor and many of the partners were products of the paralegal system. I chose my current firm because they have a really good reputation and a lot of offices.

'As a conveyancing solicitor, I currently take on 20 to 25 clients a month. It is said that moving house can be a very traumatic process for an individual and it is really important to have the right people skills where you can successfully reassure a client yet manage their expectations. Although the work is high in volume, it is crucial to remain calm and patient and take the time to explain the legal process in plain English. You must also be a good team player and help enable secretaries and paralegals who work for you to follow routines, and you need to make sure you are approachable and engaging to junior members of staff, regardless of the stress of the job.'

Office-based or in the courtroom?

Traditionally the work of a solicitor has been predominantly office-based, with some undertaking advocacy work in the lower courts (mainly criminal work in the magistrates' court). This is still mainly the case as, in practice, solicitors can earn more money working in the office than they can waiting around at court for cases to be heard. In addition, the typical hourly charge-out rates for solicitors far exceeds the average charge-out rates of barristers (for example, it is not uncommon for a junior barrister to earn £150 per day for an appearance, whereas a trainee solicitor may be charged out at over £100 per hour!) – so it is often more economical for the client to instruct a barrister to undertake court work.

Recently solicitors have been able to obtain the same right to be heard in the higher courts as barristers, known as the higher rights of audience. Once a solicitor has obtained experience of advocacy in the lower courts, they can undertake an additional training course and, upon successful completion of it, take up the higher rights of audi-ence. A number of solicitors have taken this path but it is still relatively unusual.

What makes a good solicitor?

Because solicitors deal directly with clients, perhaps the most important attribute required to make a good solicitor is excellent communication skills. Solicitors need to bridge the divide between the academic letter of the law and the practicalities of what the client is trying to achieve. The law needs to be explained to the client in terms they can appreciate and understand. Clearly, the demands placed on a solicitor in a large corporate City firm are very different from those placed on a solicitor in a high-street practice dealing with individuals, but all solicitors, wherever they work, will need:

- excellent communication skills
- the ability to cope with time pressure
- attention to detail
- good academic ability
- to be well organised
- the ability to work as a team.

Barristers

One of the complaints about the English legal system is that lawyers are like buses: as soon as one appears, another two or three turn up as well. This impression comes from the fact that solicitors can often employ barristers to give specialist advice or to represent the client in court – so, instead of hiring only one lawyer, the client now has at least two on their hands. This section will outline what barristers do and how their work differs from that of a solicitor.

What is the work like?

Barristers are specialist legal advisors and courtroom advocates: they are lawyers whom other lawyers consult on a specific issue, whether for advice or to make use of their advocacy skills. As suggested in Chapter 1, their work compares to that of consultants or surgeons in the medical profession, whereas the work of a solicitor compares more to that of a GP.

Just as the usual route to a consultant is through a referral from a GP, so the usual route to a barrister is through a solicitor (although there are a few exceptions to this – see Chapter 1, page 4): the Bar is a referral profession, so members of the public cannot generally directly engage a barrister. Solicitors will have good working relationships with barristers and are likely to know or be able to find out the most suitable barrister to deal with a particular case.

Barristers work as individual practitioners: most are self-employed and are responsible for their own caseload. They do, however, form groups, known as chambers, or sets, in which a number of barristers have their offices in the same building and share the administrative expenses of clerks and facilities – but these are not firms. Every chamber has an experienced barrister at its head; there will be a number of other members of varying seniority – permanent members of a set of chambers are known as tenants and temporary members are known as squatters.

Barristers are independent and objective, and will advise a client on the strengths and weaknesses of the case. Unlike solicitors, they automatically have rights of audience (i.e. the right to appear and present a case) in any court in the land. When a barrister qualifies, it is said that they have been 'called to the Bar', which refers to the bar or rail which used to divide the area of the courtroom used by the judge from the area used by the general public: only barristers were allowed to approach the bar to plead (argue) their clients' cases. The term 'barrister' is derived from this usage of bar. Barristers' seniority is measured in terms of their 'years of call' – i.e. how many years it is since they were called to the Bar.

There are two types of barristers: senior counsel and junior counsel. Senior counsel are those senior barristers who have been made Queen's Counsel (QC) as a mark of outstanding ability. This is also known as 'taking silk', which refers to the silk gowns they traditionally wear – thus a senior barrister is often referred to as a silk. A QC is therefore a senior barrister who is normally instructed in serious or complex cases and would usually appear only in the higher courts. Most senior judges once practised as QCs.

Junior counsel is the term used to describe all other barristers who have not been made QCs.

Barristers tend to specialise in particular areas of law, for example civil law, family law, criminal law or immigration law. The work of a civil barrister may be divided into two types: contentious and non-contentious. Contentious work involves cases where litigation is contemplated or a real possibility. Non-contentious work involves advising on matters which have arisen not from a dispute between parties but often from a desire to avoid litigation in the future (for example the drafting of a will, the creation of a trust or advising on the terms of a contract).

Why engage a barrister?

A solicitor might want to engage a barrister for two main reasons. First, to gain an opinion on a matter of law from a person who is an expert or specialist in a particular field; second, to represent the client in court where the solicitor is not allowed to or would prefer a specialist advocate to take on the task. A well-argued case will impress a judge: good cross-examination will impress a jury. A barrister's specialist advocacy skills could make a difference to the outcome of a case.

When a solicitor asks for a barrister's view on a legal point it is known a seeking 'counsel's opinion'; where the barrister is asked to undertake litigation work (for example, disputes between individuals) in court it is known as 'instructing or briefing counsel', though the two expressions are often used loosely today. If an opinion is sought the barrister will be sent the relevant paperwork and will research the area of law and consider the issues before expressing a view as to the merits of the case or what steps to take next. In many cases, barristers are able to give advice on a case simply by looking at the papers. In more complex cases, and certainly cases which go to court, it will usually be necessary to have a conference or consultation with the barrister, typically at the barrister's chambers. If counsel is instructed to act, then the barrister will begin to prepare his or her arguments that will later be used in court. Thus most of a barrister's work will typically be centred on legal disputes. The barrister acts like the old medieval champion: stepping in to fight in the place of the client.

What makes a good barrister?

'You need to have utter confidence in what you are doing – or at least appear to,' says one young barrister. 'You are absolutely vulnerable to the whims of the solicitor. You need to be flexible and robust.' A key skill for a barrister is to persuade, so strong communication skills are high on the list. You also need to be interested in people and business, and to be commercially aware (you will, after all, effectively be running your own small business). Below is a list of skills and qualities you might need:

- strong written and verbal communication skills
- confidence
- energy and drive
- the ability to think on your feet
- flexibility and adaptability
- excellent academic ability
- independence
- interpersonal skills
- meticulousness and ability to master detail
- computer skills
- commercial awareness.

Indeed, the website of the Bar Standards Board (BSB) contains a Health Warning on its website about the difficulties of getting into the barristers' profession (www.barstandardsboard.org.uk).This health warning sets out the qualities that the BSB believes are required of a barrister, which are:

- have a high level of intellectual ability
- are highly articulate in written and spoken English
- can think and communicate under pressure
- have determination and stamina and are emotionally robust.

Who works where?

There are over 12,500 barristers in self-employed independent practice in England and Wales. Although some do a wide variety of legal work, many focus on particular aspects of litigation and the law, specialising in areas such as construction, property, company law, crime, employment, personal injury, taxation, intellectual property and many other areas.

Barristers also work for the Crown Prosecution Service (CPS), the Government Legal Service and magistrates' courts. Some barristers may hardly ever appear in court but spend their time writing opinions and giving advice on complex and difficult areas of law. Most barristers practise from London but many are based in other cities and towns, including Birmingham, Bristol, Cardiff, Leeds, Manchester and Nottingham. All barristers who practise in England and Wales are members of one of the six legal circuits (geographical areas) into which the two countries are divided. The circuits are the areas around which the High Court judges travel to hear the most important cases.

Case study

Paul is an experienced barrister who has been working from chambers in London since 1985. Most of his work is with insurers, giving them advice on whether or not they should meet a claim. He deals a lot with recovery work and employers' liability.

'It is very important to build up your reputation. This often starts with your clerk who will recommend you to do a piece of work from solicitors. After that you'll tend to build up your reputation by word of mouth,' says Paul. 'Your task in court is to persuade the judge, so good communication skills are vitally important. You also need to communicate effectively with your own clients. A good grasp of the law and the enthusiasm to carry on learning is necessary.'

A lot of stamina is required to be a barrister as the job is very hard work, often requiring you to work more than 10-hour days, sometimes six or seven days a week. 'Working from 6am until midnight is common, especially on a long case which can go on for weeks on end,' says Paul. Because it is a tough profession, Paul advises that you should give it serious thought. 'It's a very enjoyable profession. For people who like to be independent and work for themselves it's the ideal profession. But you need to be able to work on your own initiative and find a way of managing your work so that it does not entirely dominate your life.' He says you need a minimum 2:1 degree and advises you to do a mini pupillage, preferably somewhere you plan to apply for pupillage.

Case study

Claire is a barrister at a large set of chambers in London, specialising in employment law. She was called to the Bar in 1998 and secured a tenancy that same year. She studied for A levels in French, Russian and Latin and then read law (European Option) at Queen's College, Cambridge, spending her third year at the University of Poitiers, France. She got a 2.i in her first year and a First in her final year. She later completed a Masters in Law at Harvard, doing a mixture of antitrust and constitutional law/civil liberties.

Before going to Harvard Claire took a year off. 'After I left college I wasn't sure I wanted to practise law, so I spent a year working for a senior barrister, doing political research and writing speeches on various topics such as human rights and discrimination. I then decided that the Bar probably was for me, so I went to Bar School.'

Claire spent time at a number of solicitors' firms in London during her university summer holidays and found this summer experience to be invaluable not only in giving her CV further credibility but also in helping her decide whether to be a solicitor or a barrister. She initially thought that she wanted to use her languages, and that being a solicitor was the only realistic option if she wanted to live abroad and still practise law as she could work from an overseas office. 'Having done a number of summer placements, however, I realised that I was perhaps not ideally suited to working in a corporate environment. I also wanted the chance, having formulated the arguments in a case, to be able to put them to a judge, and was concerned that if I did not at least try to become a barrister I might always have wondered what it would have been like. Finally, having decided, more or less on the eve of having to fill in the application forms for solicitors' firms, that I wanted to try the Bar instead, I spoke to my Dad, who suggested that the Bar was too uncertain and a bad career for a woman. There was no better way of ensuring that his extremely stubborn daughter would choose the Bar.

'While I was at Bar School I spent a lot of my time doing part-time research jobs to cover the cost of the year over and above the scholarship which my Inn had generously given me.' Claire also managed to do five mini pupillages, which were helpful both for confirming that she would like to become a barrister and also for helping her to choose where to apply for a pupillage. 'At the time I was applying for pupillage there were few chambers that were as good as my current chambers in commercial, employment and public law. Also, when I came for a mini pupillage I liked the atmosphere, particularly among the junior tenants. You need to enjoy spending time with your colleagues in every profession, but in view of the size of most chambers, and the slow rate of turnover, you have to be really sure that these are people you would enjoy going for a drink with.'

A typical day or week for Claire varies greatly depending on whether she is in court or in a tribunal – a typical week can involve a conference with a QC about the disclosure of evidence in court; drafting applications; drafting grounds of resistance; settling a long-standing case for an applicant shortly before a hearing; preparing for a judicial review; and preparing a possible injunction. There are also usually various bits and pieces of advisory work, including advising on witness statements for forthcoming hearings. Her hours are irregular and she frequently works in the evenings and at weekends.

Legal executives, paralegals and legal secretaries

Working alongside solicitors in firms are various other legal and support staff who are not fully qualified solicitors, but depending on the level of qualifications they hold may be able to carry out similar work to solicitors.

Legal executives will carry out many of the same tasks as solicitors, usually concentrating on one particular area of the law. They will therefore advise clients, carry out legal research and draft documents.

Paralegals (who may also be known as legal assistants) will work in law firms carrying out more routine legal tasks, including collating documents (for example putting together trial bundles), drafting more straightforward documents and carrying out legal research. Paralegals will often be law graduates who have not moved on to the vocational and professional stages of training. Working as a paralegal can often provide a route into becoming a qualified solicitor. The paralegal profession is currently not formally regulated, which means that it is not necessary to have any formal qualifications to become a paralegal. However, paralegals working in law firms are employed by solicitors and therefore regulated by the SRA, although in practice, the SRA usually holds the solicitors responsible if any problems occur with paralegals, as they are meant to be supervised by solicitors at all times. The Institute of Paralegals, the leading representative body for paralegals in the UK, publishes a code of conduct, which is a code of best practice. It also administers qualifications for paralegals. For more information see www. theiop.org.

Legal secretaries are basically secretaries who work in law firms – i.e. they give administrative support to solicitors. This will include taking telephone calls from clients, typing up documents and letters to clients, invoicing clients, and preparing and filing legal documents. There are no formal qualifications required to become a legal secretary, but good typing, communication and IT skills are the qualities that any firm employing a legal secretary would look for. There are several bodies offering various training courses for legal secretaries, for example the Institute of Legal Secretaries and PAs (www.institutelegalsecretaries.com).

More paralegals are being recruited to do routine work. This is often seen as a way in for law students hoping to find training contracts.

Case study

Katie began her journey towards a legal career by taking law at A level: 'I chose to study law at A level as it was an area that interested me – my cousin is a barrister and I had done some work experience with him, so was keen to do the A level as a "taster" before university. It was a really enjoyable A level as it was very different to my other subjects, and I enjoyed the problem solving element of it.'

Katie's enthusiasm for the subject meant that, when the time came to choose a degree course, she already knew that she wanted to pursue a legal career: 'I decided that the best way of doing that would be take a law degree as it would enable me to qualify as early as possible. I also liked the fact that the degree included such a wide variety of subjects that it gave me a chance to try different areas of law before specialising.' Katie read law at Southampton University.

'I looked at both the solicitors' and barristers' professions and initially had wanted to be a barrister – I think more because of the "glamour" associated with that and from seeing films and TV programmes featuring them. However, when I was studying, various solicitors and barristers would come to do talks for us and I felt that I was better suited to being a solicitor. I'm not a particularly confident public speaker and we would do mooting contests at university, which were fun but put me off the idea of standing up in court regularly. My work experience at various solicitors' firms also confirmed my preference as I enjoyed the buzz of the offices and the wide range of work involved.'

Katie applied for some vacation schemes during the holidays, but found that these were difficult to get into without some legal work experience first! However, she found other legal work experience during the summer holidays at some fairly small local firms, for one or two weeks at a time: 'This was invaluable as, while it was great studying law, you didn't get a good idea of what it would be like to work in a firm unless you saw it first-hand.'

By the time Katie had completed her Legal Practice Course (LPC), the post-2008 recession was in full swing and competition for training contracts was fierce. Many talented and qualified people were chasing too few places. Therefore, Katie learnt to touch type and found paralegal/secretarial work at a small high-street firm. 'I definitely think the legal experience I gained at this time helped me to get my training contract. The partners at my firm do look at grades when considering applicants for training, but they look just as much at work experience and any insight into the profession that people gain from having some legal work experience. During my training contract interviews, we spoke a lot about the paralegal work I had done so I think that was really important in securing the role.' Katie has also found being able to touch type a useful skill in her legal career: 'Most firms will need someone to at least be a proficient typist, whether they are working as a secretary, para-legal or fee earner, as I still do quite a bit of my own typing!'

Katie is now a conveyancing solicitor at the firm where she did her training contract, a medium-sized regional firm. 'I chose this firm because of its reputation in the local area – I wanted to work at a well-respected firm of a decent size. It had also received awards for training and I therefore felt it would provide me with a good start to my career.

'I qualified into conveyancing which is a busy area. It is a fast-paced job and often stressful, but I enjoy the work as it is intellectually testing at times and varies day to day. I enjoy working with people and have a large amount of client contact, which I really love. I also enjoy working as part of a team and we have a great team of people within our office.

'You need to be well organised, to be able to cope well under pres-sure and to have excellent communication skills – these are all things that I have developed while on the degree and during my training.

'I have certainly benefitted from all of my legal work experience and my advice to all law students is to just get as much as possible on your CV as it is one thing that can make you stand out from the crowd when applying for training contracts. A lot of the people I went to law school with joined firms straight after the LPC to get some experi-ence and ended up getting their training contracts that way, rather than applying directly for a training contract without any experience.'

The legal profession in Scotland

The main difference in the composition of the legal profession in Scotland is that instead of there being the two separate professions of solicitors and barristers, in Scotland there are solicitors and advocates.

Solicitors

As in England and Wales, solicitors in Scotland give advice on a wide variety of areas of law, with individual solicitors specialising in particular areas. Solicitors in Scotland can represent clients in the Justice of the Peace and Sheriff courts.

Solicitors in Scotland are both represented and regulated by the Law Society of Scotland, which sets standards for the profession, including education and training requirements, and disciplines solicitors where necessary.

Solicitor advocates

Solicitor advocates are experienced solicitors who have extended rights of audience and can also appear in the High Court of Justiciary and the Court of Session. They are members of the Law Society of Scotland and are regulated by that body.

Advocates

Advocates (sometimes referred to as 'counsel') are lawyers that are specifically trained in advocacy, so can represent clients in any Scottish court. They are equivalent to barristers in England and Wales, and the relationship between solicitors and advocates works the same as that between solicitors and barristers in England and Wales, in that advocates are usually instructed through a solicitor instead of being instructed directly by individuals.

Advocates are members of the Scottish Bar, and are regulated and represented by the Faculty of Advocates, which carries out similar functions as the Law Society of Scotland does for Scottish solicitors.

Reform of the legal profession in Scotland

The Legal Services (Scotland) Act 2010 made various changes to the operation of the legal profession in Scotland. It aims to reduce the restrictions on solicitors entering into business relationships with non-solicitors, as the Legal Service Act 2007 has allowed solicitors, barristers and non-lawyers to work together in England and Wales. However, the introduction of so-called alternative business structures in Scotland has been long delayed due to a failure to introduce an appropriate regulatory structure.

> For more information on the legal profession in Scotland see www. lawscot.org.uk and www.advocates.org.uk/about-advocates.

The legal profession in Northern Ireland

As in England and Wales, the legal profession in Northern Ireland is divided into the two distinct branches of solicitors and barristers, and these professions have the same roles as in England and Wales. Solicitors in Northern Ireland are represented and regulated by the Law Society of Northern Ireland, and barristers are regulated by the General Council of the Bar of Northern Ireland.

> For more information please see: www.lawsoc-ni.org/about-us and www.barofni.com.

4 | How to qualify as a lawyer

So now we come to the crucial matter: how do you start on the long road to becoming a lawyer? As there are two distinct branches of the legal profession, there are different training routes for each branch. This chapter will start by looking at how to qualify as a solicitor in England and Wales, followed by an overview of how to qualify as a solicitor in Scotland and Northern Ireland, and will then move on to qualifying as a barrister in each of the three jurisdictions.

Solicitors: England and Wales

It may come as a surprise to learn that there are a number of different routes by which you can qualify as a solicitor. Most of these are set out in the diagram on page 39 and then described in more detail in the text that follows.

Before university

A levels

A wide range of A levels provide an acceptable grounding for a law degree and there are no specific subject entry requirements to be able to study law at university. The traditional essay-based subjects such as history and English have an obvious appeal: they involve assimilating and analysing information, and a significant amount of writing, which will all be required on a law degree course. Languages may also prove to be very attractive to employers, particularly if you end up working for a firm with offices overseas, and sciences will develop logical thought and application, which are key skills for any lawyer. Many universities do not accept either General Studies or Critical Thinking A levels at all for any of their courses.

The leading Russell Group of 24 top UK universities publishes a document called 'Informed Choices' which provides advice and guidance on choosing A level subjects (www.russellgroup.ac.uk/informed-choices.aspx). This document contains a list of what are termed 'facilitating subjects', which are all the traditional academic subjects:

- maths and further maths
- English (literature)
- physics, chemistry and biology
- history and geography
- languages (both modern and classical).

The Russell Group universities recommend that potential applicants to these universities choose at least two of their A levels from this list of facilitating subjects. This will keep a wide range of degree courses open to them. Aspiring lawyers should be aware that studying for a law degree involves a considerable amount of reading and research, requiring a high degree of literacy. Therefore, if you choose all maths and science A levels and then wish to study law at university, you may need to be able to demonstrate to your chosen university that you possess the level of literacy and essay-writing skills required on a law degree. This could possibly be done by careful comments in the personal statement on the UCAS form (see Chapter 7, pages 79–88) or perhaps by taking an Extended Project Qualification (EPQ) – an additional qualification, which requires you to undertake a self-directed period of research, which is then usually written up in a dissertation. This can be related either to one of your current A level subjects or to your future career.

Whether or not an aspiring lawyer should choose A level Law seems to cause some controversy. The obvious advantage of taking law at A level is that it will provide you with an introduction to the subject and give you some idea of what studying law is like and whether or not it appeals to you before you have to commit to studying law at university.

There have been suggestions in the press that A level Law is a 'soft' subject, not favoured by universities, and it is not on the Russell Group list of facilitating subjects. However, research published by the exam board AQA suggests that, in reality, this is not the case generally.

In March 2014, AQA published a document entitled 'In support of A level Law. Universities don't like A level Law – fact or fiction?'. This document quotes from the A level Law reviews of 2009 and 2010 and also includes comments by law admissions tutors from some top universities, including the University of Cambridge. The conclusion reached was that a large majority of the country's top universities treat A level Law like any other A level, and studying it confers neither an advantage nor a disadvantage when it comes to applying for a law degree. Some even see it as an advantage. The document includes a (long) list of universities which confirmed that A level Law is an acceptable entry qualification for their law courses.

However, it is still important to bear in mind that A level Law is not a facilitating subject for Russell Group universities and, for example, the London School of Economics and Political Science (LSE) specifically states on its website that at least two traditional academic subjects are preferred and that law is a non-preferred subject.

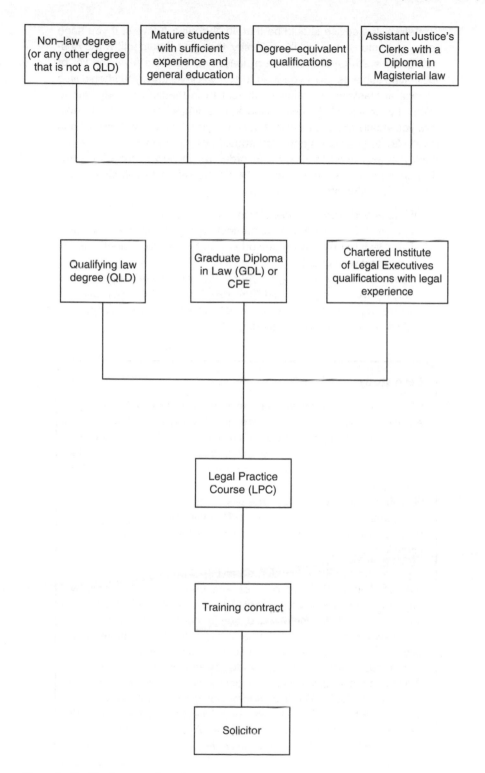

Figure 1: Qualification route for solicitors

Therefore, the advice should be that, in choosing A levels, if you hope to go on to study at a top UK university, then you should follow the Russell Group's advice and choose at least two subjects from the list of facilitating subjects. So if you wish to study A level Law, you should also choose at least two traditional subjects from the list to study with it. With all your A level choices, including deciding whether or not to take law, you should choose a subject because you think you will enjoy it and it will play to your strengths. You should not choose law because you think that you need to study it in order to go on to study for a law degree, as this is not the case. To be on the safe side you should also take the following steps:

- If you already have a university in mind, check with the admissions section of its website what its particular entry requirements are and, if you wish to take law (or any other non-facilitating subject), whether or not it will accept it.
- If you are already studying for your A levels but have not yet chosen which universities you would like to apply to, then do your research before applying so you know which universities will accept your combination of A level subjects.

Case study

Elly always knew that she had an interest in law: 'Initially I had ambitions to join the police force but decided I could find more intellectual challenge in a career as a solicitor. I studied A level Law for two reasons: firstly, I wanted to find out whether I actually enjoyed studying law and to ensure it was the area I wanted to commit to. Secondly, I wanted to ensure I could cope with the challenges the law provides. The law is often illogical and frustrating; some people simply cannot get on with these challenges so they never have the opportunity to explore the ideas and opportunities in the law.'

Elly went on to take a law degree at the University of Exeter and graduated in 2015. She did not encounter any reluctance by her chosen universities to accept A level Law and believes her A level Law provided a useful foundation for her degree studies: 'In A level Law you only study very small areas of the law compared to a degree. For these particular areas (crime and tort for me) my A level was invaluable and certainly gave me a head start in these modules. A level Law also gives you an understanding of how to approach and deal with the law and this understanding is undoubtedly required in every module taught at degree level.' She also believes that work experience before university is helpful: 'A university degree is a huge commitment and if you can show the university you are able to make this commitment through work experience then you are going to be more successful in being offered places at top universities.'

Elly also made sure that she did work experience while at university: 'I believe it is vitally important to have legal work experience to show your commitment to the law – no law firm wants to offer a training contract to a student who is likely to drop out to do something else. I undertook two mini pupillages and four vacation schemes. This may seem excessive to some but each firm is different and it was as much for me to learn about the firm as it was for getting experience on my CV.'

The work experience also helped Elly decide whether she wanted to become a solicitor or a barrister: 'Initially I did want to be a barrister, but having done two mini pupillages with barristers I felt there was not enough client contact and that cases were picked up and dropped easily. I wanted to build long-term professional relationships with clients and do more than just represent them in court.'

Elly has been offered a training contract at a medium-sized firm of solicitors in the City of London and will start this once she completes her LPC: 'I chose my firm based on the work they did and the "feel" of the firm. It is difficult to get a training contract because the quality of candidates is so high. The type of law firm you want to get a training contract with will determine how difficult it is to get a training contract. I was rejected more times than I care to count, but in the end I ended up with four offers and I accepted the firm I felt fitted me the best in terms of the work undertaken, the type of people I would be working for and with, and the atmosphere at the firm.'

Access to Higher Education courses

If you are a mature student who missed out on completing your secondary education, and can not satisfy university entry requirements, Access to HE courses are designed to help you move into higher education and on to degree-level studies. Most access courses are delivered in further education colleges (although some are available at certain universities) and are available across England and Wales. The courses can be taken in a range of different subjects and lead to the Access to Higher Education Diploma, which is widely recognised by universities.

To find out more about Access to HE courses, visit the Access to Higher Education website (www.accesstohe.ac.uk), which contains further information on the Diploma and a link to a database of further education colleges offering Access courses.

Some employers will particularly welcome applicants who have had some 'life experience' in other fields before starting their legal career and the skills and qualities that more mature applicants offer can be much valued. This will be the case more for some employers than others (the civil service and teaching profession are good examples), although all employers must disregard age in their recruitment decisions to avoid breaking anti-age-discrimination laws. However, you should research carefully the legal career you are interested in before embarking on the expensive and time consuming training to becoming a lawyer.

Academic stage of training

Law degree

Many universities offer law degrees, and these vary to some extent in style and content – for example:

- some are more traditional and 'academic' in approach
- some are slightly more vocational in outlook
- some enable you to obtain a joint degree (e.g. law and languages, law and politics, law and accountancy).

This variety gives you the opportunity to choose the degree which best suits your skills and interests – but if you have any intention of qualifying as a solicitor, you should ensure that your degree is recognised by the Solicitors Regulation Authority (SRA) as a qualifying law degree (QLD) – see Chapter 6, page 68 for details. The SRA maintains a list of certain institutions and the degrees they offer that are recognised as QLDs, so it is easy to check whether your preferred degree is on the list. Having a QLD means that you have studied the subjects which the SRA considers to be the core foundation subjects for any lawyer.

These are:

- contract
- tort
- criminal law
- public law (including constitutional law, administrative law and human rights law)
- land (or property) law
- equity and the law of trusts
- law of the European Union.

The Law Society stipulates that, for a degree to constitute a QLD, the study of legal subjects must account for not less than two years out of a three- or four-year course of study (i.e. 240 credits in a 360 or 480 credit degree programme). At least half of a normal three-year degree course (i.e. 180 credits) must be spent on the foundation subjects listed above. Some study of legal subjects must also take place in the final year of the course. The SRA also stipulates that the teaching methods must allow students to acquire knowledge and understanding of the fundamental doctrines and principles which underpin English law. Once you begin looking for a training contract (see below), you will discover that many firms will expect you to have either a First or 2.i degree. You will need to work hard right from the outset of your degree to maximise your chances of getting a training contract with the firm of your choice.

Non-law degrees: the Graduate Diploma in Law (GDL)

What do you do if your degree is in a subject other than law and, during or on completion of your studies, you decide that you wish to qualify as a lawyer? In this case, you would need to obtain an additional post-graduate qualification, which is usually known as the GDL – although some universities and colleges (and indeed the SRA) still refer to it by its former name: the Common Professional Examination (CPE). This qualification is accepted by both the Bar Council and the SRA, so, subject to the need to apply for vocational training places as early as possible (see below), you could start the GDL without having decided whether you eventually intend to qualify as a solicitor or as a barrister, and then make your decision during the course of your studies.

The GDL is a condensed programme of study, usually comprising a one-year full-time course offered at around 50 universities and law schools across England and Wales. Many of the same institutions also offer the GDL on a part-time basis over two years. Part-time online distance learning programmes are also available. As with qualifying law degrees, the SRA maintains a list of all institutions that offer the GDL (available at www.sra.org.uk/students/courses/cpe-gdl-course-providers.page).

Application for a full-time GDL course is made via the Central Applications Board (the CAB), which runs an online system similar to UCAS (see Chapter 7), acting as a hub for all full-time applications for the GDL and LPC (see below). Up to three different institutions can be applied to at once. Its website is www.lawcabs.ac.uk. There are no application deadlines for the CAB, which simply recommends that candidates should apply at their 'earliest convenience', but it does advise you to check on the individual course providers' websites for application closing dates as they may not accept late applications. Applications for part-time or distance learning GDL courses are made direct to the institution(s) of your choice.

The current cost of a full-time GDL ranges from around £3,500 to around £10,000. You should check what the course fee includes – for example, some providers will include the cost of all books and materials within their fees, whereas others will expect you to pay for these direct. You should also investigate the amount of contact time offered by the different course providers. Remember that you often get what you pay for, so do not necessarily opt for the most inexpensive course. Try to talk to some students who are currently studying or have previously studied at the institution you are interested in to find out whether they were happy with the course. You should also consider where you would like to do your training contract, as certain law firms favour certain law schools. For more information on funding the GDL, and the choice of institution for the GDL and LPC, please see below.

Case study

Mark was always very clear about his career aspirations but decided that in order to have the option of specialising in intellectual property he needed to complete a science degree as some of the work can involve patents and scientific know-how. He studied chemistry at Imperial College and spent two years in London and two in Paris, where he undertook research and studied French literature. Mark then applied to do his CPE at the University of Law in London.

'I wanted to move back to London after Paris and wanted to be at the University of Law, because it has a reputation for quality courses and is well recognised by leading firms. I had already started doing vacation placements at various firms and knew that although I enjoyed the research, long-term I wanted to work in a profession more oriented around people.'

Mark found the CPE very fast paced and practical, which is excellent for a scientist who has always dealt with the practical applications of his experiments. 'CPE students do miss out a little on discussing the implications of law, but the practical aspects are great and really prepare you for life in a law firm.' Mark had always been part of a debating team through school and university, and when he arrived at law school he was keen to help give the debating team a boost. 'Debating introduces you to the skills of presenting your case in a logical way and in public. All solicitors need these skills as they have to talk to clients, think on their feet and justify their actions in an ordered and coherent way.'

Non-graduate route

If you do not possess a degree, there are still a number of options available to you. You may apply to the SRA for a certificate of academic standing which will allow you to apply for the GDL course. This is granted by the SRA if it is satisfied that you hold other academic or vocational qualifications that it considers to be equivalent to a degree. Briefly, the situations where this may be possible are:

- **Mature students.**
  If you have a considerable amount of experience (normally at least 10 years) or have shown exceptional ability in an academic, professional, business or administrative field and have been educated to at least A level standard, and have a good command of English, the SRA may issue a certificate to allow you to take up a place on the GDL course.
- **Assistant Justices' Clerks.**
  Assistant Justice's Clerks who have gained a Diploma in Magisterial Law are usually eligible to take the GDL, and may even be granted exemptions from some of the papers.
- **Chartered legal executives.**
  Those already working in the legal sector, for example as a paralegal, could take the Chartered Institute of Legal Executives' examinations during a period of qualifying employment. These qualifications are recognised by the SRA as being equivalent to a law degree and therefore enable you to progress to the next stage of training, the LPC (see below) without obtaining a degree.
- **Degree-level qualifications.**
  These may include professional accountants' or surveyors' qualifications.

More information on the non-graduate route to qualification is contained in the Academic Stage Handbook, which is available on the SRA website. If in any doubt, you should contact the SRA, whose staff will be able to give you advice on your particular circumstances.

Vocational stage of training

Legal Practice Course (LPC)

Following completion of the academic stage of training, aspiring solicitors must complete an LPC at one of around 35 universities and law schools across England and Wales. The LPC can be completed over one year full-time or two years part-time (in a variety of formats including day, evening or weekend study patterns). The current cost ranges from around £10,000 to around £15,000 for the full-time course. The yearly fees are less for the part-time courses.

The LPC is made up of a combination of compulsory and elective modules. The compulsory modules cover the subjects and skills in the core practice areas, and you must cover these regardless of where you take the LPC. You also take three elective modules which you will be able to choose from the range offered by your chosen course provider. Different institutions offer different elective subjects, so when you apply for the LPC, you should make sure that you choose courses that offer the elective modules you are interested in. These should be modules that cover areas of law that you would like to work in in the future.

The larger solicitors' firms that offer help with fees for the LPC (see page 48) often only do so if you study for it at one of their preferred course providers and take the optional modules that are most relevant to their areas of practice. For example, if you intend to work in the City as a corporate lawyer, you will need to take commercial law options. BPP University has strong ties to the leading firms in the City and is the exclusive course provider for trainees from over 50 leading law firms. The University of Law is the preferred training provider for over 30 more law firms. You need to make sure that you take the LPC at the institution preferred by the law firm you would like to work at.

The LPC is very different from the academic stage of training: it is based on legal practice rather than theory; you will spend a lot more time in small groups with other students and the skills content of the course means you will experience much more 'learning by doing'.

As with the GDL, applications for a full-time LPC course must be made via the Central Applications Board (www.lawcabs.ac.uk). Again, the CAB does not have application deadlines for the LPC, but you should check with the institutions individually to see whether they have their own application deadlines. Applications for part-time courses are made direct to the institution(s) of your choice.

Exempting degree

The idea behind the exempting degree is to combine the academic and vocational stages of training. At the time of writing, only six exempting law degrees are on offer and the universities which offer these are listed on the SRA's website (www.sra.org.uk/students/exempting-law-degrees.page). The degrees are four years long and, on completion of your studies, you'll be deemed to have the equivalent of both a QLD (see page 42) and the LPC. The obvious attraction of the exempting degree can be the funding arrangements.

Training contract

The final stage of your route to qualification as a solicitor is the training contract. This is (usually) two years of on-the-job training with a firm or other organisation which has been authorised by the SRA to take trainee solicitors. The purpose is to enable you to understand the practical implications of the law as well as developing your legal skills. The SRA requires you to gain experience in at least three distinct areas of law during your training contract and to further develop your legal skills while doing so. You should spend at least three months working in each of these areas. You will also have to complete the Professional Skills Course (PSC), which includes further training and some assessment in legal skills. Your firm or employer is expected to support you through this process and must pay your fees and reasonable travel expenses.

Depending on the sort of firm you want to go to for your training contract, you may need to apply up to three years in advance of your possible start date. This is certainly the case with the large City and national corporate and commercial firms, which will be recruiting as you are entering either the penultimate or the final year of your degree studies or starting your GDL. The application deadlines vary from firm to firm – some recruit earlier than others and some only have relatively short windows in which they will accept applications in any one year. Most recommend applying early. Other firms and organisations will recruit you as you are completing your LPC, with a view to an immediate start, so it is also common for students to start their LPC without knowing if they have a training contract to go to at the end of the course. There is a voluntary Code of Good Conduct for the recruitment of trainee solicitors, which represents good practice in legal recruitment. Law firms are not obliged to follow this Code, but most will in practice. The Code is available on the Law Society's website and specifies, among other things, that the opening date for training contract applications must not be earlier than the penultimate year of your undergraduate study. You can not be required to accept or decline any offers before 15 September in your final undergraduate year.

You can complete your training contract on a part-time basis and you can also combine your training contract with attendance on a part time LPC. If you have considerable previous work experience in a legal environment, then you may be eligible for a reduction in the length of your training contract of up to six months, but this will depend on whether your employer supports your request. Any application has to be made to the SRA.

Competition for training contracts is fierce. The number of training contracts registered annually has remained at around 5,000 since 2009–10. In the year to July 2014, the number was 5,001, whereas 6,171 students completed their LPC course in the academic year 2012/2013. Following the advice in this book should put you in the best possible position to obtain a training contract – also consider your A level choices carefully and obtain the best grades you can; consider your choice of university carefully – there is some evidence that the top firms still look to what they perceive as the 'good' universities for their trainees. Finally, enrol on some vacation schemes and try hard to obtain some relevant work experience (see Chapter 5 for more details).

Students completing the LPC (2012/2013)	6,171
New training contracts started (2013/2014)	5,001

Table 2: Competition for solicitors' training contracts

Funding your qualification

Qualifying as a solicitor, therefore, has become an expensive business and it's not unusual for students to find themselves in tens of thousands of pounds of debt at the end of their LPC. So, what are your options?

Sponsorship

Most of the larger firms will sponsor you through the LPC and possibly the GDL if you have secured your training contract before commencing the course. The sponsorship will cover the cost of the GDL/LPC course fees and usually a contribution towards your living expenses as well. You'll need to check whether the firms that interest you would offer sponsorship of this kind. Firms providing sponsorship deals often do so on the proviso that you take your LPC at their preferred university or college. This is so that they can make sure that you study the subjects that they will need you to know about once you start working for them.

Law Society Diversity Access Scheme

The Law Society has a Diversity Access Scheme (DAS), which is aimed at students from disadvantaged backgrounds or those who face exceptional obstacles to qualification. Its purpose is to increase social diversity in the legal profession. The DAS offers payment of LPC course fees, plus the provision of work experience and a professional mentor. The scheme is, however, limited: in 2015, the Law Society offered ten standard DAS awards. Competition for awards is keen and applicants must have a confirmed place on the LPC. More details are available on the Law Society's website (www.lawsociety.org.uk/law-careers/diversity-access-scheme).

Career development loans

Once you get to the LPC stage of training, you may be eligible for a career development loan. These are deferred repayment loans offered by certain banks to fund vocational training courses. The Government pays the interest on the loan while you are studying and you the repay the loan once you start working. For more information see www.gov.uk/career-development-loans.

Access funds and scholarships

These are available at some universities offering the LPC. Access funds may be available at publicly funded colleges and are discretionary awards aimed at assisting with your living costs if you are experiencing financial hardship. Scholarships may be awarded by any of the universities or colleges offering the LPC to students with particularly good academic backgrounds. Details are available direct from your institution of study.

Payment by instalments

Some institutions where you can take the LPC course offer the option to pay by instalments. You should check the institutions' individual websites for details.

Charities and grant-making trusts

Some grant-making trusts and charities may offer financial assistance to those seeking to qualify as a lawyer. You should search online to see whether there are any such bodies in the area where you live and, if there are, check whether you meet their criteria for an award. These are usually very specific, so that eligibility is extremely limited.

Study part-time

More and more students are completing their professional training part-time, mostly due to the lack of financial support. This will enable you to work part-time to help support yourself. You should, however, make sure that you allow yourself enough time to study so that you pass the course.

Funding: conclusion

When you are looking for sources of funding, remember:

- do your research
- plan ahead
- read the criteria for any grant/award you are applying for very carefully and make sure you can demonstrate that you meet them
- don't be put off – you're hoping to train to be a solicitor so try to come up with a good case for yourself
- be realistic.

Case study

Karen took A levels in English language, law, mathematics and general studies and then went to Bristol University, where she read law. In her first year she studied tort, criminal, public and property law. In her second she chose jurisprudence, contract, property, trusts and European law. In her third she elected to do medicine, law and ethics, intellectual property, revenue law, and gender and the law. She obtained a 2.i.

Karen was clear from the start that she wanted to be a solicitor: 'I wanted to be able to deal with clients from the beginning of a case and because of the possibilities for solicitor advocates nowadays it didn't seem to be closing any doors. I also dislike the stuffy traditions of the Bar.'

Karen made sure that she gained work experience through summer work placements. 'After my second year at university I spent an intensive summer working for three different large London solicitors' firms for two weeks each. I also spent a week in an in-house legal department.' Karen found a training contract at a medium-sized law firm based in the City of London.

Karen chose to train at a medium-sized firm with a reasonably large number of trainees partly because of the good in-house training the firm provides for its trainees: 'There is a good induction

---

programme and a comprehensive system of support, so there is always someone to help you when you need it.' However, because of the intense competition for training contracts Karen thinks you need something to help you stand out. 'Being outgoing, having a sense of humour, and language and computer skills will give you an edge,' she says. 'My legal experience also helped enormously.' She advises: 'You must be very committed before going to law school as costs are great unless you are sponsored. Be focused and persistent.'

Solicitors: Scotland

As outlined in Chapter 2, the legal system in Scotland differs from that of England and Wales and Northern Ireland, and so does the qualification route. It is not possible to go into great detail in this book but below is a summary.

Briefly, the route to qualification involves studying for a four-year law degree at a Scottish university and then proceeding to the vocational training stage. There is no equivalent of the GDL in Scotland, so it is slightly more difficult to become a lawyer if your degree is in a subject other than law, as this necessitates taking a two-year accelerated law degree after your first degree. Further details on qualifying in Scotland are available on the Law Society of Scotland's website (www.lawscot. org.uk/media/555081/Overview-of-route-to-qualification.pdf).

Academic stage

Law degree

It is possible to study a Bachelor of Law degree (LLB) at the following Scottish universities:

- The University of Aberdeen
- The University of Abertay
- The University of Dundee
- The University of Edinburgh
- Edinburgh Napier University
- Glasgow Caledonian University
- The University of Glasgow
- Robert Gordon University
- The University of Stirling
- The University of Strathclyde.

More detailed information about the content of the law degrees can be obtained from the law schools at each of the universities by visiting their websites.

The law degrees are honours degree courses, which in Scotland are studied over four years. Students who already have a degree in another subject can apply for a two-year accelerated degree.

> Warning: A law degree from an English university will not be accepted as a QLD in Scotland, and vice versa. However, if you have qualified in England, Wales, Northern Ireland or other parts of the European Union, there are transfer tests available in order to requalify in Scotland. Information on how to convert qualifications from a different country (e.g. if you qualified in England but want to practise in Scotland) can be found by visiting the websites of the law societies and bar councils for each country.

The non-graduate route

Alternatively, there is a non-degree route where someone who has been working as a full-time pre-Diploma trainee with a qualified solicitor in Scotland for three years can take the Law Society of Scotland's examinations and then proceed to the vocational stage of training in the same way as a law graduate. This route is known as the Pre-PEAT Training Contract and LSS exams, and, according to the Law Society of Scotland, is followed by between 10 and 20 people each year. For more information please see www.lawscot.org.uk/media/555081/Overview-of-route-to-qualification.pdf

Vocational stage

Diploma

After completion of the LLB degree all aspiring Scottish solicitors are required to take the Diploma in Professional Legal Practice (DPLP) which is also known as the Professional Education and Training Stage 1 (PEAT 1), which is usually taught full-time over one academic year and can be studied at six Scottish universities. Some two-year part-time courses are also available. This is the equivalent of the LPC in England and Wales, in that the course has been designed to teach the practical knowledge and skills necessary for the working life of a solicitor. The focus is highly practical and skills-based. To obtain a place on the diploma course, applicants would need to have passed all of the Law Society of Scotland's 'professional subjects' in their LLB (or Law Society examinations). Applications are made direct to the universities offering the course.

Training contract

After successful completion of the degree (or non-graduate route) and diploma, you need to serve a two-year post-diploma training contract

(Professional Education and Training Stage 2, or PEAT 2) with a practising solicitor in Scotland. This can be served with solicitors in private practice, the Crown Office, or local authorities and certain public bodies. The training contract is very similar to that in England and Wales, giving trainees the chance to put into practice what they have learnt at university. At the end of the two years, if the training contract has been successful then the trainee is qualified and can apply for a full practising certificate. As in England and Wales, competition for training contracts is intense and there are now fewer trainee roles available for a similar number of students passing the DPLP. A good academic profile is therefore important and the benefits of having obtained some work experience, particularly in the legal sector, can't be over-estimated.

Solicitors: Northern Ireland

The system for qualifying as a solicitor in Northern Ireland is different again from those in England, Wales and Scotland. Below is a brief summary, but further details can be obtained from the Law Society of Northern Ireland's website (www.lawsoc-ni.org/joining-the-legal-profession/).

Academic stage

The usual route to qualification as a solicitor in Northern Ireland begins with a law degree. This must be considered by the Law Society of Northern Ireland to be a 'recognised law degree', and must contain eight core subjects. Further details of what constitutes a recognised law degree, and a list of recognised law degrees and the universities offering them, are available on the website of the Institute of Professional Legal Studies, part of Queen's University Belfast (the 'Institute'). This list of recognised law degrees contains many from English and Welsh universities, as well as some in the Republic of Ireland, so this part of the route to qualification does not have to be taken in Northern Ireland. Degrees in Scottish law are not, however, recognised.

Students with non-law degrees can also qualify as a solicitor by first taking the Masters in Law at Queen's University, Belfast.

There is also an alternative, non-law degree route available. Please visit the website of the Law Society of Northern Ireland (www.lawsoc-ni. org/joining-the-legal-profession/) for further details.

Vocational stage and apprenticeship

The vocational training to become a solicitor in Northern Ireland (the Postgraduate Diploma in Legal Practice) is undertaken at the

Institute. The Graduate School of Professional Legal Education, part of the University of Ulster, also used to offer postgraduate legal training, but is scheduled to close in the first half of 2016 and therefore courses are no longer being offered there. All applicants applying for the diploma must sit an entrance exam in the December before they wish to commence the course (known colloquially as the 'Institute exam'). Applications must be submitted to the Institute by 15 November in the relevant year. The main difference from the system in England and Wales is that applicants must have already found a master (a solicitor with whom the applicant proposes to serve his/her on-the-job training, known as the apprenticeship) by the time they apply for the vocational course. The vocational course is then combined with the apprenticeship. Finding a master can be a difficult and competitive process.

The apprenticeship is similar to a training contract in England and Wales, in that it will last for two years for trainees who completed the traditional qualification route. However, in order to combine it with the vocational training, each year is structured as follows.

- September to December: spent in-office.
- January to December: spent at the Institute of Professional Legal Studies (but returning to master's office during vacations).
- January to August: spent in-office.

Once a trainee has passed all the relevant examinations and completed their apprenticeship, they can apply to be enrolled as a solicitor of the Court of Judicature in Northern Ireland and apply for a Practising Certificate. A restricted practising certificate is issued for the first two or three years, meaning that newly qualified solicitors can only practise as employees.

For more information on qualifying as a solicitor in Northern Ireland, please see www.lawsoc-ni.org/joining-the-legal-profession.

Barristers: England and Wales

Academic stage

The academic stage of training required to become a barrister is the same as that required to become a solicitor. It is only once a student reaches the vocational stage of training that the qualification routes for solicitors and barristers diverge. Please see the section on qualifying as a solicitor for details on A levels, law degrees, and the GDL. A good academic background is even more important for aspiring barristers than it is for solicitors: it is going to be very difficult to obtain a pupillage (see below) unless you achieve at least a 2.i at degree level.

Vocational stage

Bar Professional Training Course

To become a barrister entitled to practise, the Bar Council requires you to take the one-year (full-time) or two-year (part-time) Bar Professional Training Course (BPTC), previously known as the Bar Vocational Course (BVC). A partial distance learning course is also available. Before registering on the BPTC you will need to be admitted to one of the four Inns of Court: Gray's Inn, Inner Temple, Lincoln's Inn, or Middle Temple (all based in central London). These Inns provide support for barristers and student members, advocacy training and other continuing professional development opportunities, lunching and dining facilities and access to common rooms and gardens. The Inns are also responsible for Calling barristers to the Bar, which is the mechanism by which students become barristers once they have completed the BPTC and pupillage (see below).

The BPTC aims to help you gain the knowledge of procedure and evidence and skills of advocacy, conference skills, drafting, legal research, negotiation and opinion writing to prepare you for the practical stage of training on the job, the one year of pupillage. The BPTC is available at 13 different teaching institutions throughout the country:

- BPP University (Birmingham, Leeds, London and Manchester)
- The University of Law (Birmingham, Leeds and London)
- Cardiff Law School
- City Law School
- Manchester Metropolitan University
- Nottingham Law School
- The University of the West of England, Bristol
- The University of Northumbria at Newcastle.

Applications for the BPTC must be made through the centralised applications system run by the Bar Student Application Service, which has an online application form (www.barsas.com). The system opens for application in the November before the anticipated year of entry and the closing date is usually in the following January. You should check online for the exact closing date. An application fee of £58 is payable.

Bar Course Aptitude Test (BCAT)

In 2013 the Bar Standards Board introduced the Bar Course Aptitude Test (BCAT) which applicants for the BPTC have to pass before their offer of a place on the BPTC can be confirmed. The purpose of the BCAT is to test applicants' critical thinking and reasoning, which are considered to be the core skills required for the BPTC. The idea is to make sure that students starting the BPTC have the necessary skills to pass it.

This is another hurdle for potential barristers to overcome. The fee for taking the test is £150 if it is taken in UK and EU test centres and £170 for non-EU test centres. For more information on the BCAT, including a practice test so that you can familiarise yourself with the type of questions asked, visit www.barstandardsboard.org.uk/qualifying-as-a-barrister/bar-professional-training-course/bar-course-aptitude-test/.

Pupillage

Pupillage is the final stage to qualifying as a barrister and is hard work. The first six months of pupillage (known as the 'first six') are non-practising and involve training with a senior barrister (your 'pupil supervisor') at work for six months. During the first six months you will be expected to undertake legal research, draft opinions, and read your pupil supervisor's paperwork.

Once you have completed the first six months, you will spend the second six months (the 'second six') practising and be able to appear in court as an advocate. This is when you start to build your own reputation and have your own cases. Pupils must be paid a minimum salary of £12,000 per annum, plus reasonable travel expenses where applicable.

Those of you eager to become a barrister are in for a tough time. Competition for places is very keen. The Bar Standards Board website even includes a Health Warning to warn about the intense competition for pupillages. It reports that around 1,700 students take the bar course every year, whereas the number of pupillages available in each year is only around 480. To make things even tougher, students are allowed to try to find a pupillage for up to five years after completing the bar course, so in any one year, there could be over 3,000 people applying for pupillages. Some barristers' chambers report having over a hundred applicants for each pupillage placement. Even if you are successful in obtaining a pupillage, there is no guarantee of work after completing it – in every year, there are usually fewer tenancies available at chambers than there are students completing their pupillages, and the opportunities for employed barristers are few and far between. The Bar Standards Board recommends undertaking thorough research to find out if a career at the Bar is really for you, and this includes making a realistic assessment of whether you have the capacity to become a good barrister.

| Students completing BPTC each year | 1,700 (approx) |
| Pupillages available each year | 480 (approx) |

Table 3: Competition for barristers' pupillages

Applications for pupillage are made through an online pupillage application system, called 'Pupillage Gateway', which is operated by the Bar Council. The system allows applicants to search and apply for pupillage vacancies. All pupillage providers must advertise all pupillage vacancies on the Gateway. There is a common timetable for the application process and no charge is made to applicants. For more information, visit www.pupillage-gateway.com.

Before applying, you should find out as much as possible about your preferred set of chambers. You should study the chambers' website carefully and look at online bar directories. You should also try to attend a pupillage fair. These are held every so often to enable students who wish to pursue a career at the Bar to meet different sets of chambers.

Case study

Emma is a barrister at a large set of chambers, based in London, and specialises in personal injury cases. She took a somewhat convoluted route to the Bar. 'I studied psychology, philosophy and music for A level. I didn't put in nearly enough effort and my grades were not what they should have been, which I suspect hampered my applications for pupillage later on.' After a degree in drama at Loughborough, Emma obtained a Masters in Chinese Law, Politics and Mandarin from the School of Oriental and African Studies (SOAS).

'I had always been told I would be a good lawyer, but I didn't understand what the job involved. I don't have any lawyers in my family and I thought I would have to represent people accused of serious crimes. What I didn't appreciate is that you can be a lawyer without ever doing a criminal case. It wasn't until I was studying for my master's that I started to understand what being a lawyer involved. Initially I wasn't sure whether I wanted to be a solicitor or a barrister but work experience very quickly made things clear for me. My first mini pupillage was a whirlwind of excitement, whereas I kept falling asleep when I did work experience at solicitors' firms! Most people tend to know pretty quickly which role suits them better.'

Having obtained the necessary academic qualification in law by taking the GDL, Emma obtained an Outstanding for the BVC (now called the BPTC). 'The difficult part was getting a pupillage. I worked as a paralegal on very poor pay for one year after Bar school in order to improve the legal experience section on my CV. I ended up giving up paid employment altogether for a month in order to focus on ensuring I had time to take on some Free Representation Unit work that I felt would bolster my CV. Showing that you are dedicated to the legal profession and that you understand what it involves is crucial when it comes to pupillage applications.'

Emma tends to be in court most days, be it for a five minute application or an all-day trial. On top of that, she has various Advices, Particulars of Claim or Defences to draft. 'The hours vary. Being organised and efficient in your working habits is very important if you want to keep a work/life balance. While I often work in the evenings and weekends, I'm always home for supper, find time for lots of sport and manage to have drinks with friends fairly regularly.'

Emma believes that the skills required to be a barrister vary depending what area of law you specialise in. 'It is very important for all barristers to be well prepared for a case. However, in my line of work cases often change at the last minute or you only get instructed at 6 p.m. the night before a 10 a.m. hearing. A flexible approach and an ability to respond to last minute issues is crucial, as is being able to perform damage limitation when things go wrong. Being polite, pragmatic and generally decent towards judges, court staff and other barristers also goes a long way.'

Funding your qualification

The average cost of completing the vocational stage of training is estimated at over £20,000 if living expenses are taken into account. The fees for the BPTC for 2014/2015 were between £12,000 and £18,000 for the year. Only a limited number of awards, grants and scholarships are available for the vocational stage of Bar training. The Inns of Court offer a range of scholarships and some chambers give awards towards the BPTC. However, the majority of students have to depend on bank loans or other forms of support. Please refer to the individual chambers' websites or the Bar Council website for further details.

Advocates: Scotland

The academic and vocational stages are the same as qualifying as a solicitor in Scotland (see the section on qualifying as a solicitor in Scotland on page 50). The intending advocate in Scotland needs to take a law degree followed by the postgraduate Diploma in Professional Legal Practice plus a minimum of 21 months' training in a Scottish solicitor's office.

This is followed by nine months' further unpaid practical training called 'devilling' (work-shadowing) which involves working as a pupil for an experienced practising advocate (a 'devilmaster'), in combination with sitting the Faculty of Advocates' written examinations. Please visit the Faculty of Advocates website for more information: www.advocates. org.uk/about-advocates/becoming-an-advocate/information-for-students.

Barristers: Northern Ireland

Details on how to qualify as a barrister in Northern Ireland are available on the website of the Bar of Northern Ireland (www.barofni.com/page/ becoming-a-barrister). Very briefly, the academic stage is the same as for qualifying as a solicitor; students must have completed a recognised law degree (see the section on qualifying as a solicitor in Northern Ireland on page 52).

For the vocational stage of training, students must complete the one year full-time Bar Postgraduate Diploma in Professional Legal Studies at the Institute of Professional Legal Studies, Queen's University, Belfast (the IPLS).

After graduating from the Institute when they have passed the Bar course, students are called to the Bar of Northern Ireland. Bar trainees must then undertake a pupillage with a master for a period of 12 months.

5 | Getting work experience

Getting work experience is crucial in terms of helping you secure a training contract or pupillage in today's extremely competitive climate. It is not enough to be purely a brilliant academic. The more relevant experience you have, the better the chance of succeeding.

You can apply for work experience at any stage in the qualification process, whether it be during A levels, during a law (or other) degree, or even at a later stage if you are having trouble obtaining a training contract or pupillage. There are many types of vacation schemes run by the larger firms of solicitors and chambers also offer mini pupillages. These are invaluable ways of gaining experience and getting a foot in the door. You will be much more attractive to potential employers if you can show that you have some legal work experience. Most of these work experience schemes are only available to undergraduates.

However, having some work experience is also very useful in applying to university for a law degree. You are less likely to be able to find a place on a formal work experience programme while you are still at school, but you should still look for some sort of experience just to get you into a legal environment and see what lawyers actually do. This will support your application for a law degree and help you write the personal statement on your UCAS form (see Chapter 7, pages 79–88).

What have you got to gain from work experience?

- It will give you an insight into the profession and whether or not it is what you want to do. Some real experience will be particularly useful if you are trying to weigh up the pros and cons of qualifying as a barrister or solicitor or, if the latter, which type of law firm you would prefer to work in.
- It gives you something to write about in your application for legal jobs (or a law degree) to show that you are serious about entering the legal profession and have done your homework to make sure that it is really for you.
- It gives you the opportunity to build up those all-important contacts.

- It will help you to gain excellent references (hopefully!).
- It helps you to make a better transition to your eventual move into the world of full-time work.

However, it is not that easy getting legal work experience, and can in itself be a competitive process. Most universities and employers recognise this and do not stipulate that work experience is essential, although it is preferred and you should try hard to do some. If you can't get experience in a firm of solicitors or chambers, any work experience that demonstrates use of the skills they are interested in will be valuable. Skills such as communication, determination, business awareness and IT can all be developed in many other sectors of business and commerce. Even just showing that you can get up every day and present yourself for work at 9 o'clock in the morning is of some use.

There are also other ways of gaining relevant legal experience while you are at school or university, for example, participating in a debating society or in mooting or mock trials will help hone your advocacy skills. Some university students hoping to enter the legal profession volunteer at their university law centre or law clinic.

If you look through the case studies contained in this book, it is noticeable that all the young lawyers did a variety of work experience while at school and university, and they all think it played an important part in landing them a job at the end of their studies.

Where to apply for work experience

Law firms' vacation schemes for aspiring solicitors

The big corporate law firms offer a range of different vacation schemes, and if you are at all interested in this type of law, you should apply for some of these. If you are interested in commercial law, but do not necessarily want to train at one of the biggest firms, it is still useful to have done one of these vacation schemes as it will impress any smaller commercial firm that you may apply to for a training contract by showing that you have done your research into working as a commercial solicitor. Even if you are not sure what type of law you are really interested in (or, indeed, whether you would like to become a solicitor or barrister) it is worth applying for some of these schemes as it may help you make up your mind.

There are different sorts of schemes depending on what stage of your education you are at and whether or not you are studying law at university. Many firms offer shorter 'taster' schemes for first year undergraduates, followed by slightly longer schemes (of two, three or four weeks) for students in their penultimate year of university. The same schemes may be open to those taking a non-law degree, or different schemes may be available. Most take place during the summer, but some are available during other university holiday periods. To research these vacation schemes, you need to look at the websites of all the big law firms (some of which are listed in Chapter 3). There are often strict application timetables that require you to apply up to a year in advance (so, for example, in the first term of the academic year for a placement the following summer).

Generally, vacation schemes pay a small amount of money to cover your expenses while you are there. Many of these big firms link their vacation schemes to their training contracts. You may not necessarily have to do a vacation scheme to be offered a training contract, but it will certainly help, and some firms use vacation schemes as a way of finding suitable candidates to offer training contracts to. Some firms recruit trainees almost exclusively from their vacation schemes. They will also give you a genuine insight into the culture of the different firms and help you decide where you would like to work. One junior solicitor commented that she only applied to firms that she had done a vacation scheme with as she knew much more about what they were like and whether she would enjoy working there.

Mini pupillages at chambers

Similarly, many barristers' chambers offer mini pupillages, which allow you to shadow a practising barrister for up to two weeks to find out what working as a barrister is really like. If you think that there is any possibility that you might like to become a barrister, then it is crucial to try hard to undertake a mini pupillage. You can search online for barristers' chambers that offer mini pupillages and there are also online search tools available, such as at www.lawcareers.net.

Where else to apply

- Placement in a firm of solicitors that does not offer a formal vacation scheme
- shadowing court officers
- shadowing a barristers' clerk
- voluntary work at a Law centre
- Citizens Advice Bureau
- voluntary work in other charitable organisations.

Looking through the case studies (and example personal statements) contained in this book will also give you some ideas.

Try as many ways of getting work experience as you can think of and be creative in the process. Here are a few suggestions.

- Ask your teachers at school/college if they have any contacts in the legal profession.
- Use your careers service and speak to your careers officer.

- Talk to your family and friends and ask them if they can suggest anyone to contact.
- Make sure everyone you know is aware you are looking for work experience.
- Make direct approaches to firms of solicitors that do not offer formal vacation schemes. The Chambers and Partners or Legal 500 online directories (see Chapter 12, page 112 for details) will give you names and addresses of solicitors' firms.
- You can also approach sets of chambers that do not offer formal mini pupillage schemes. The Chambers and Partners directory will also give you names and addresses of chambers.

While you are trying to get work experience, you should make sure that you keep up to date with current affairs relating to the legal world and the legal profession by reading a quality broadsheet newspaper and looking at specialist journals such as *The Law Society Gazette* and *The Lawyer*, which should both be available from large public libraries and are also online (see Chapter 12, page 117 for details).

You should ask to go in for one or two weeks' work experience during the holidays or even just ask for one day's work-shadowing to get an insight into what the working environment is like. Anything that anyone is prepared to give you will be useful. Whichever route you take will almost certainly be unpaid unless you have specific skills to offer, such as good office and keyboard skills. If you can touch-type, you could try to get some paid work with a firm of solicitors during the summer or register with an employment agency.

How to apply

CV

Many formal vacation schemes and mini pupillages will require you to apply online using an application form. For anything else, you will probably need to put together a CV to support your application. This is a summary of what you have done in your life to date. If you have hardly any work experience then one page on good-quality A4 paper will be sufficient. If you are a mature student with a lot of jobs behind you there is sometimes a case for going on to a second page. So what should go into your CV? Here are the main headings:

- name
- contact details
- education and qualifications
- previous work experience.

There is no standard CV but there is a sample opposite. Make sure to include the following points. You should ensure that you don't leave

A sample CV

PERSONAL DETAILS
Simon Anthony Tate
134 Hillhouse Avenue
Portsmouth PO1 2TQ
01234 567890
simontate@btinternet.com

EDUCATION & QUALIFICATIONS
2007–present: Linfield High School, Portsmouth
A levels: English, History, French
GCSEs (June 2012): English Language (A), English Literature (B), Mathematics (B), History (A), French (A), Latin (A), Chemistry (B), Biology (B), Physics (C)

WORK EXPERIENCE
August 2012: Two weeks as a temporary receptionist in a small firm of accountants, responsible for answering telephone and general clerical work
2011 & 2012: (Saturdays) Sales Assistant in busy dry cleaners in centre of Portsmouth
2010 & 2011: Delivering newspapers and magazines throughout my local area

SKILLS
Languages – good written and spoken French
Computing – competent in MS Word and Excel

POSITIONS OF RESPONSIBILITY
Captain of football team at school

INTERESTS
Football, swimming, reading (particularly Jane Austen), and travelling to other countries such as America and France

REFERENCES
Mr. T. Smith
Head of Sixth Form
Linfield High School
Portsmouth
tsmith@linfield.org.uk

Mrs A. Whiting
Hugg & Co. Accountants
47, High Street
Portsmouth
a.whiting@huggs.co.uk

any gaps and account for all your time. Also, if something such as illness prevented you from reaching your potential in your exams, point this out in the covering letter (see below). Lawyers have excellent attention to detail, so make sure your spelling and grammar are perfect!

Education

Start with your present school, college or university and work back to the beginning of secondary school. No primary schools please! List the qualifications with grades you already have and the ones you intend to sit.

Work experience

Start with the most recent. Don't worry if you've only had a Saturday job at the local shop or a paper round. Put it all down and try to draw out any relevant skills you have gained from it. Employers would rather see that you've done something.

Skills

List those such as computer skills, software packages used, languages and driving licence.

Interests and positions of responsibility

What do you like to do in your spare time? If you are or have been captain of a sports team, been a committee member or even head boy or head girl at school, put it all down.

Referees

Usually two: an academic referee such as a teacher or head of your school plus someone who knows you well personally, who is not a relative, such as someone you have worked for.

Covering letter

Every CV or application form should always be accompanied by a covering letter. The letter is important because it is usually the first thing a potential employer reads.

Here are some tips:

- The letter should be on the same A4 plain paper as your CV and should look like a professional document. No lined paper please! One side of A4 only.
- Employers accept typed letters, unless they specifically request one to be handwritten.
- Find out the name of the person to whom you should send your letter and CV. It makes a great difference to the reader if you can

personalise your application. If you start the letter 'Dear Mr Brown', remember you should finish it 'Yours sincerely'.

- The first paragraph should tell the reader why you are contacting them and what stage of your education you are at.
- The second paragraph should give them some brief information to make them interested in you, e.g. highlighting your interest in law, along with some specific IT skills.
- Thirdly, you should explain why you are applying to them, for example interest in their line of work, desire to experience work in a small/large firm/set, etc. Mention anything you already know about the firm/chambers and make sure that it is correct. Look carefully at their website and make sure you know what area of the law they practise in!
- Check very carefully for spelling and grammatical mistakes.

A sample covering letter is shown below.

Dear Mr Smith,

I would be very interested in applying for some work experience at Smart & Shady LLP, and wondered whether you have any such opportunity available. I am currently in the first year of my law degree at Sussex University, and would relish the chance to gain some practical experience during the forthcoming summer break.

From looking at your website I can see that Smart & Shady has an outstanding reputation for dealing with high-value commercial transactions, and this is an area of law that I am particularly interested in, having chosen to study commercial law as an option in my second year.

As part of my degree, I have become proficient at conducting legal research. I also have strong IT and typing skills, as well as good communication skills that I have built upon by taking part in debates at university.

Please do not hesitate to contact me if you require any further information or would like me to come to your office to meet you in person.

Yours sincerely,

Simon Tate

Case study

Laura studied law and criminology at The University of Kent, Canterbury, graduating with a 2.i.

'During my time at university I took part in several activities that I thought interviewers would focus on when I began looking for work after law school. I worked part time at the university Law Clinic. This only took up a few hours every fortnight but allowed me to gain practical experience of working within a functioning law firm as well as developing my ability to work alongside professionals and interacting with clients. I undertook several other periods of work experience, including a mini pupillage. Each period of work experience helped me to decide which area of law I would eventually like to work in as well as allowing me to make important contacts within the profession. Along with my housemates I also started a social society that raised lots of money for charities, and during training contract interviews this was always commented on.

'During my LPC year, I volunteered at the local domestic violence centre, which developed my ability to deal sensitively with clients. I also used the careers service, which helped me to prepare my CV and to practise my interview techniques. I also applied for several jobs advertised on their website. I was then offered a training contract with one of these firms, which then led to a full-time position in their criminal department.

'Although good academic results are obviously important I cannot stress how important it is to show a keen interest in the area you wish to work in, show willingness to invest your time and treat every period of work experience or voluntary work as an interview.'

Bury College
Millennium LRC

6 | Choosing your university law course

This chapter focuses on how to go about choosing a law degree. The aim is to produce a shortlist of degree courses you are interested in and from that to choose the top five courses to put down in your UCAS application.

As previous chapters have made clear, you do not need a law degree to enter the legal profession. Equally, a law degree can be an excellent springboard into a wide range of other careers. Employers are generally impressed by a good-calibre law graduate, since law is known to be a challenging discipline requiring skills such as research, analysis, application, clarity, advocacy and effective written communication. These are relevant in many other careers as well as those in the legal professions.

If you do not wish to read law at university, most of the advice in this chapter will still be relevant to choosing your degree course, but for more general advice on choosing degree courses, please refer to some of the guides mentioned in Chapter 12.

What to consider

The basic criteria for choosing your degree course are:

- the type of law course you are interested in
- your academic ability
- where you want to study.

Most of the information you need to know about universities and the courses available at them is available online either through:

- UCAS (www.ucas.com)
- universities' own websites. Most universities have their prospectuses available to download online (although you can request a paper copy to be sent through the post if you prefer) and there should also be information on who to contact if you have a specific question.
- university comparison guides and league tables such as the Complete University Guide (www.thecompleteuniversityguide.co. uk) and the Guardian University Guide (www.theguardian.com/

education/ng-interactive/2015/may/25/university-league-tables-2016). There are also books providing similar information, such as *The Times and Sunday Times Good University Guide*. Make sure you use the most up-to-date edition.

Going to university is an investment, particularly with the rise in tuition fees in recent years, so the choice of what to study and where to apply to must be given careful thought. You will also spend three years of your life there, so you will want to make sure that you will be somewhere you will enjoy living. There are many institutions offering law courses and you will need to look at ways of narrowing down your options.

Types of law degree

Many law degree courses are offered by many different institutions across the country and the choice may at first appear daunting. However, the range of options can quickly be narrowed down once you know what you are looking for. The important thing is to choose the right course for you. The key points to consider are:

- If you intend to qualify as a solicitor or a barrister in the future, the degree must be a qualifying law degree (QLD) if you wish to go straight onto the LPC afterwards.
- Should you choose an LLB or a BA (and does it matter?)?
- Should you choose a single or joint honours degree?

Qualifying law degrees

Qualifying law degrees are recognised by the Law Society and the Bar Council, and only QLDs allow students to progress to the vocational stage of training. This means that you do not need to spend an extra year taking the GDL after you graduate. A list of the institutions that offer QLDs and lists of the different courses they offer can be found at www.sra.org.uk/students/courses/qualifying-law-degree-providers.page. All qualifying law degrees will cover the following seven core subjects (sometimes referred to as the seven foundations of legal knowledge):

1. contract
2. tort (often referred to, with contract, as obligations)
3. criminal law
4. public law, including constitutional law, administrative law and human rights law
5. property law (or land law)
6. equity and the law of trusts
7. law of the European Union.

The Glossary contains an explanation of these terms. You will also learn about legal research techniques and the English (or Scottish or Northern Irish) legal system.

As is explained in Chapter 4, for a law degree to constitute a QLD, the Law Society requires you to study legal subjects for at least two-thirds of the time (for a three year degree course). At least half of a normal three year degree course must be spent on the foundation subjects listed above. This means that there will be a lot of similarities between QLDs as they all spend half the time, at least, on the above subjects. However, the rest of the course content, and the range of optional subjects available, will vary considerably. The style of teaching and the approach taken to studying law will also vary (see below for more information on different approaches to studying law).

LLB or BA?

Some law degrees are classified as LLBs, whereas others are BAs. As a broad generalisation, LLB degrees will involve spending all of your time studying law, whereas a BA or BSc degree may involve spending some time studying non-law modules. However, so long as the degree is a qualifying law degree, all the core legal subjects will still be covered, and whether you end up with an LLB or BA will not affect your ability to pursue a legal (or any other) career. For historical reasons, the universities of Oxford and Cambridge do not award LLBs at all and their law degrees are BAs. If you are interested in studying non-law modules as part of your law degree (for example, foreign languages), then the increased breadth may well be interesting and valuable for you and also welcomed by future employers.

Single or joint honours?

Law can be taken on its own (a single honours degree) or mixed with one or more other subjects (a joint honours degree).

A single honours degree will allow you to focus on studying law, although some courses will also permit you to take individual modules from other subject areas; even from completely different disciplines. As well as the core subjects, you will also be able to choose optional subjects (particularly in second and later years). Some institutions can offer only a limited selection of options, while others provide a much greater variety. If there is a particular area of law you are interested in, for example intellectual property law, then you may want to apply to a university that offers this as an option.

A joint honours degree will allow you to divide your time between law and one or more other disciplines. Usually, where two subjects in a degree title are joined by the word 'and', this indicates that the course will involve a 50/50 split between the two subjects, whereas the word 'with' suggest a two-thirds/one-third split. However, this is a broad generalisation and you should always check the details of any particular course on the university's website. A joint honours degree course must satisfy the Law Society's requirements if it is to qualify as a QLD (see above), so it is likely that joint honours degrees that are QLDs involve spending more than half the time studying law. A popular combination is to study law with a European language, although you should note that these courses often specify that candidates must have an A level or at the very least a GCSE in the relevant language.

It is important to check that any joint honours degrees in particular are QLDs (see above) if you want to go on to be a solicitor or barrister and want to make sure that your degree will satisfy the academic stage of training so that you do not need to spend an additional year taking the GDL.

Approaches to teaching law

It is interesting to note by way of background that there are broadly three different approaches to teaching law – but you cannot base your selection on this criterion since few institutions adhere to one kind. Most places are likely to opt for a mixture (sometimes even within an individual unit, especially if it is taught by several different tutors). However, the emphasis of different law schools may be different. The approaches are:

- *Pure academic approach*. This approach focuses on the core legal subjects and doesn't look much beyond statutes and law reports for its sources of law. It provides a thorough grounding in the relevant legal system and its laws.
- *Contextual approach*. Law can also be examined in context; that is to say, law, its role and its effectiveness are looked at in relation to society (past and present), politics and the economy. This approach may include elements of critical legal theory. Students are expected to analyse the problems (for example, loopholes, contradictions, injustices and so on) within the law. This can make for some heated and controversial seminars.
- *Vocational approach*. This stresses professional training and skills such as negotiating, interviewing, counselling, drafting, research, analysis, clear expression and the ability to read through vast amounts of material, sift out the legally relevant points and present a logical argument. These skills are mainly covered during the vocational stage of training to become a solicitor or barrister, but may also be looked at in a law degree. Extra-curricular activities such as mooting (a mock courtroom trial), debating and law clinics, in which students get the opportunity to help out with a real-life case from start to finish, also help develop these skills at university.

Academic requirements

Entry requirements for law degrees vary greatly, both in terms of the standard that they expect students to have achieved and also in how they are expressed. You will need to research which degrees at which universities your likely A levels, Scottish Highers, IB or BTEC qualifications will enable you to access. It is important to be realistic about the grades you are likely to achieve: don't be too pessimistic, but don't kid yourself about your 'as yet undiscovered' genius. Talk to your teachers for an accurate picture of your predicted results. You can then target your universities accordingly. Don't forget that you need to select one or two universities with lower grade requirements than your predictions as 'insurance' choices.

Most of the top universities offering QLDs require applicants to have three A levels (or their equivalent) and the grade requirements have become even more challenging since the introduction of the A* grade. The most selective universities, for example, Cambridge, now regularly include the A* grade in their offers. Information on the entry requirements for law degrees at different universities is available through UCAS or the websites of the universities themselves.

Less academically selective universities often express their entry requirements as a target number of UCAS points using the UCAS Tariff system. This system is used to allocate points to the different qualifications taken by students before they access higher education. It therefore allows students with different types of qualifications to access undergraduate degree courses, and also allows the universities to compare applicants with different qualifications. It is important to note that the UCAS Tariff system is in the process of changing and the new system will be used for courses starting from September 2017, based on a different number system. The purpose of the new system is to accommodate the reforms to qualifications currently being introduced (such as the new A levels) and also to enable more vocational qualifications and more international qualifications to earn points, thereby supporting political demands for widening participation. The new UCAS Tariff tables (as well as the existing tables) are available on the UCAS website.

Your A level subject choices may also have a bearing on which universities you can realistically expect to receive an offer from. Few courses specify subjects they want you to have studied (with the exception of most language joint degrees), although qualifications in traditional academic subjects are preferred at the more selective universities and are welcomed everywhere. Some universities won't accept A levels such as general studies or critical thinking, and possibly even the less academic ones such as art. No institutions require A level Law from potential students. See Chapter 4, pages 37–40 for more information on A level subject choices. You should always check carefully on the websites of all the universities you are interested in to confirm their specific requirements.

If your predicted A level results (or chosen A level subjects) effectively prevent you from taking a law degree, then it's time for a rethink. If you wanted to take a law degree with a view to entering the profession, then you could opt for the non-law degree entry route instead. Most employers stress that a large number of trainee solicitors and pupil barristers have a non-law degree. Remember that if you read a subject other than law, you will have to complete the GDL before going on to the LPC or BPTC. The disadvantage is that the route might be longer and therefore more expensive (if sponsorship cannot be found).

Choosing a university

Once you have made a realistic assessment of your likely A level grades (or other qualifications) you can think about choosing specific institutions. Remember, university life isn't going to be solely about academic study. It is truly a growing experience – educationally, socially, culturally – and besides, three or four years can really drag if you're not happy outside the lecture theatre. Here is an assortment of factors which might help you to choose where you would like to study. Some of these will be more important to you than others, so you should use the paragraphs below to think carefully about the things that matter most to you.

Warning: different legal systems

If you're hoping to practise law, then you must be sure where you intend to work within the UK (i.e. England or Wales, Scotland or Northern Ireland). Since the legal systems differ throughout the UK, you must qualify in the part of the UK you intend to practise in in the future. If you did subsequently decide to move, then it would usually be possible to convert qualifications from a different country (e.g. if you qualified in England but want to practise in Scotland). More information can be found by visiting the websites of the Law Societies and Bar Councils for each country, mentioned in Chapter 3. More detail on the differences between the professions in each of the UK countries can be found in Chapters 2 and 3.

Open days

Attend university open days if you can, visit the law departments and talk to former or current students and course lecturers and tutors. If you can not attend any open days, there are often campus tours available, or you can make an independent visit. Try to go on a taster course for law at any university if possible. This does not need to be a university to which you are actually thinking of applying – even if it is not, it will still give you an idea of what to look for in universities in general and will also give you something to mention in your personal statement (see Chapter 7, pages 79–88).

Types of university or college

There are a number of ways of categorising universities and higher education colleges, but there are two broad categorisations by which these institutions are often sorted:

Old or new?

Almost all law degrees are taught by universities and these can be categorised as 'old' or 'new'. A few other colleges of higher education also offer law degrees:

1. 'Old' universities. Traditionally the more academic universities with higher admission requirements, the old universities are well established, with good libraries and research facilities. They are well respected by employers and provide an academically rigorous training.
2. 'New' universities. Pre-1992, most of these were polytechnics or institutes of higher education and these generally still hold true to the original polytechnic doctrine of vocational courses and strong ties with industry, typically through placements and work experience. Their approach to teaching law may generally be slightly more vocational in nature. They can still be looked down upon by some employers because of their generally lower academic entry requirements, but many of the new universities have a good name for flexible admissions and learning and modern approaches to their degree teaching. There are also some private universities, such as BPP University, the University of Law and Buckingham University. These universities can offer even greater flexibility in the way your degree course is structured. Some private universities now offer the chance to take a degree that would normally take three years in only two years of full-time study, which can be really helpful if you want to qualify as quickly as possible, and possibly of particular interest to mature or overseas students. You will simply forgo the long holidays usually associated with university degree courses. Private universities tend to be more vocational in their approach. They receive no state funding, so are not subject to the Government's cap on tuition fees, but may not necessarily be more expensive, especially if you choose the two-year degree option. Some institutions offer part-time degree courses.
3. Colleges of higher education. Usually these are specialist institutions and therefore provide good facilities in their chosen fields, despite their size. They are sometimes affiliated to universities, which means the college buys the right to teach the degree, which the university will award, provided that the course meets the standards set by the university.
4. The Open University, which is a very well-established provider of part-time distance-learning degree courses, offers an LLB degree that is a qualifying law degree.

City or campus?

Universities are also often divided into campus or city universities. So, when looking at which university to choose you need to consider whether you would prefer to live on a university campus, surrounded by your fellow students and the university's facilities, or whether you would prefer to be more integrated into town or city life. The choice is slightly more sophisticated than this broad division, since many universities offer something of a mix between these two extremes. For example, there are campuses in the middle of, or right on the edge of, cities or towns. Other campuses are practically surrounded by open fields and the nearest town or city is a bus ride away. Some city universities are largely contained in one area, whereas others are spread throughout the city.

The town or city where the university is based, particularly its size, can also have a big effect on the 'feel' of the place. So, for example, some city universities have a largely separate university area, but are close to the centre of a large city (for example, Leeds). Others are more inte-grated into the city (such as Sheffield). Some have a largely self-contained campus, but are still in a big city (such as Nottingham). Universities more often thought of as campus universities may be more likely to be near a smaller town than a big city (for example, Lancaster and Warwick).

Other factors to consider

Attractiveness to employers

Few employers will openly admit to giving preference to graduates from particular universities. Most are looking for high-quality degrees as an indication of strong academic ability. But since students with higher A level grades have tended to go to the older and more prestigious univer-sities, it is unsurprising that a large proportion of successful lawyers come from these universities. Employers are often so swamped with applications that they use university background as an easy way to filter applicants, reckoning that the better universities will have picked the higher-calibre students and therefore have done part of their job for them. It therefore makes sense to be aware of the reputations of the different universities (which can often be gleaned from their position in the league tables) and factor this into your decision. You must obviously choose to go somewhere that you will enjoy, but since (at least part) of the object of the exercise is to find a good job at the end of your univer-sity studies, it is foolhardy to ignore how potential employers will view your degree.

Quality of teaching

This is difficult to establish without the benefit of an open day, and even then you will only have the opportunity to meet one or two of the teach-ing staff and speak to one or two students. However, league tables of universities for each subject are published by several organisations, such as the *Guardian*, the *Times and Sunday Times* and *The Complete University Guide*. The *Guardian University Guide 2016* for law is avail-able online at www.theguardian.com/education/ng-interactive/2015/

may/25/university-league-tables-2016 and the Complete University Guide 2017 Law league table is at www.thecompleteuniversityguide. co.uk/league-tables/rankings?s=Law. *The Times/Sunday Times Guide* is available in print format and is published annually.

The National Student Survey is conducted each year to get feedback from students who have studied at university, and is more focused on overall student satisfaction. Scores are given for many factors, including the quality of teaching and how good teachers are at providing feedback to students. The results of the survey are published online, including at www.hefce.ac.uk/lt/nss/results and on the website of Unistats: unistats. direct.gov.uk/find-out-more/about-the-data. Since the raising of tuition fees, students have become a lot more interested in issues such as teaching quality and 'contact time' — i.e. how much face-to-face teaching you will actually get, and it makes sense to investigate this as much as you can.

Teaching quality may suffer if seminar or tutorial groups are too large, so try to also compare group sizes for the same courses at different institutions.

Educational facilities

Most universities should have a well-stocked and up-to-date law library. They should also have good-quality IT resources and fast broadband internet connections. More vocational courses might also use mock courtrooms with video and audio equipment. The facilities available will depend on the budget of an institution, and obviously how they choose to spend it. You may want to look at the law department at the university. Is it in the new, shiny, state-of-the-art building or a dilapidated 1960s monstrosity hidden from view? At the end of the day, university is about more than just buildings – academically, the quality of teaching is more important and non-academic factors will also make a big difference to whether or not you enjoy your time there. However, if you are concerned about the environment in which you study, you should investigate the building housing the law department.

Non-academic considerations

- **Finances.** The cost of living differs substantially throughout the UK, so will you be able to reach deeper into your pockets for rent or other fundamentals and entertainment if you are living in a major city or in the south? If you are living in London, you will need particularly deep pockets.
- **Distance from home.** Do you want to get away from your family and friends or stay as close to them as possible? While there can be advantages, financially at least, to living at home if you go to your local university, you may prefer the challenge of looking after yourself and the opportunity to be completely independent. Also think about whether you want to be able to go home at weekends without spending half a day (or more) on a train.

- **Accommodation.** What sort of accommodation is on offer? Do you want to live on campus or in halls of residence with other students, or in private housing that you may need to organise yourself that could be a considerable distance from college? Most universities provide accommodation for first year students at least, but how far this is from the teaching areas of the university will vary. You may simply be able to roll out of bed and totter next door for your 9am lectures, or you may be looking at a half-hour bus journey in rush hour. Some universities offer accommodation beyond the first year, which will save you having to live in private housing.
- **Catering.** Would you prefer to go somewhere where you can have your meals cooked for you, or are you keen to unleash your inner chef and cater for yourself?
- **Interests.** Will the university allow you to pursue your interests? Are you going to be spending much time in, for example, the sports centre, the theatre or student bars? How about university societies: is there one that allows you to indulge your existing hobbies or the ones you've always dreamt of trying? Most universities have a huge choice of extra-curricular activities and entertainments and very good facilities. However, you should think about exactly what is provided, the standard of participants and whether all abilities are catered for (are you a county squash player or simply keen to have a go?) and how far the facilities that you will want to use are from the accommodation or teaching areas. Some universities have particular reputations for particular extra-curricular activities – for example, Loughborough for sport.

Studying overseas and work placements

The opportunity to study overseas and/or complete a work placement could also be factors affecting your degree selection. Some universities will allow you to go to an overseas university with whom they have an arrangement for one year of your studies. Others will allow you to spend a year in the middle of your degree on a work placement. You do not need to be a linguist to study abroad, since you can study or work overseas in English in, for example, North America, the Netherlands or Malaysia. The availability of student exchanges has increased through programmes such as Erasmus (an EU student exchange programme), which encourage universities to provide international opportunities where practicable. If you are planning to study law at university, these opportunities may be more limited, as law is a very jurisdiction-specific subject.

Similarly, few law degree courses offer work placements during your degree. You will usually need to arrange this for during university holidays (see Chapter 5, pages 60–61).

7| The UCAS application and the LNAT

So you have chosen a few universities that you would like to apply to for a law degree; now what? This chapter will guide you through the UCAS application process for a law degree, and then give you some advice if you are applying to any universities that require the LNAT entrance exam.

Suggested application timescale

Lower Sixth

January onwards. Start doing some serious thinking and begin researching degree courses. Get ideas from friends, relatives, teachers, books, etc. Investigate (and book) one-day taster courses run by certain universities, for example, London (see http://tasters.gradsintocareers.co.uk) and work experience for the summer holidays (see Chapter 5, pages 60–61).

April. Find out when open days are being held (you may have to request universities you are interested in to notify you when bookings open). See www.opendays.com. Many are held in late June/July (after summer exams) and then again in September/October. It is helpful to do some in June/July if possible.

June/July. Attend open days. Look at university department websites, download prospectuses and department brochures.

July/August. Make a shortlist of your courses. Try to do as much research as possible over the summer holidays. This is particularly important for applicants to Oxford and Cambridge. Also, undertake work experience and wider reading (see suggestions in Chapter 12). Start writing your personal statement. Review your courses shortlist when you receive your summer exam results.

Upper Sixth

September onwards. Finalise your personal statement and UCAS form, then complete your application and send it off to UCAS. Register and book a place to sit the LNAT if you are applying to a university that uses it (see below).

15 October (6 p.m. UK time). Deadline for submitting your UCAS application if you are applying for places at Oxford or Cambridge.

20 October. Deadline for sitting the LNAT if you are applying to Oxford.

December. Interviews for Oxford and Cambridge are held.

15 January (6 p.m. UK time). Deadline for submitting your application to UCAS. They will consider late applications, but your chances are limited since some of the places will have gone already.

February–April. Interviews at non-Oxbridge universities may be held.

25 February – 4 July (6 p.m. UK time). If you have received decisions from all five of your choices, and were either rejected or have declined the offer you received from all of them, you can enter UCAS Extra, a scheme that allows you to apply to other universities, one at a time. See the UCAS website (www.ucas.com) for details.

November – March. Decisions (and hopefully, offers) arrive.

31 March. By this date, universities and colleges are encouraged to send UCAS their decisions on all applications received before 15 January

4 May. If you have received all your university/college decisions by 31 March, assuming you've had some offers, you must tell UCAS which offer you have accepted firmly and which one is your insurance choice by this date.

June. Sit your exams.

August. (Third Thursday) Results day. If you got the grades, well done! UCAS will send you confirmation of your place. If you missed your grades, don't be too disappointed. Clearing starts straight away so don't waste any time – get hold of a list of unfilled places and contact the universities direct. You will be sent instructions on Clearing automatically. UCAS has now introduced a new scheme called Adjustment which allows students who have performed significantly better than they had expected a short period of time to approach universities that require higher grades than the offer they were holding. See Chapter 10 for more information on your options on results day.

The UCAS form

The online UCAS form is accessed through the UCAS website (www.ucas.com). Most applicants register through their school or college, but it is possible to register independently. The UCAS form has six sections that you need to fill out.

1. Personal details: name, address, nationality, etc.
2. Choices: universities and courses you wish to apply for and your proposed year of entry.

3. Education: including exam results and exams to be taken.
4. Employment: including part-time work.
5. Personal statement: see below.
6. Reference: this is usually written by your school or college, but independent candidates can ask employers or other contacts to act as a referee.

> General advice on filling in your UCAS application is given in another guide in this series, *How to Complete Your UCAS Application* (Trotman Education).

Your personal statement

The personal statement is the most important part of your UCAS application and is your opportunity to demonstrate that you are fully committed to studying law and have the right motivation and personal qualities to do so successfully. It is therefore vital that you think very carefully about how to complete it so that it shows you in the best possible light. You need to sell yourself to the law admissions tutors. It will take time and effort to get it right, so you must allow yourself plenty of time and not attempt to rush it. Expect to go through many drafts before you come up the final version that you are happy with.

There can often be over 20 applicants per place at some universities offering law degrees, so applying for a law degree is very competitive. A good personal statement can help you to stand out from the crowd and persuade an admissions tutor to give you an offer rather than one of the other equally well-qualified applicants.

Obviously, there are as many ways of writing a personal statement as there are candidates. There are no rules as such, but you should try to follow the following advice.

The personal statement should cover three key areas.

1. Why you want to study the course for which you are applying.
2. Why you would be good at the course and are well qualified to embark on it.
3. What other interests you have and (if possible) what transferable skills they give you which would be relevant for the course.

Section 3 should not make up more than 25% of the statement (or even less for the most academically competitive universities, such as Oxford, Cambridge and LSE). The focus should be on your academic interest in the courses applied for, and why you are a good candidate, and in most cases this should account for around 75% of the statement.

Some key points to remember are:

- The personal statement must be no longer than 4,000 characters (including spaces); this is a strict limit, so you need to ensure that you are within it.
- Write in your own words. The statement must be honest and personal and it must sound like you.
- Use evidence. Don't make broad-brush statements, but focus on what you have **actually done** and what you have learnt from it. Focus on how what you have done has helped you to decide a law degree is for you or to become a good candidate for a law degree.
- Check and re-check the statement for spelling, punctuation and grammar. Even better, ask a parent, teacher or family friend to do this for you.
- Do not over-use superlatives ('passion' etc) although you should sound enthusiastic and committed.

Why you want to study law

The first part of the statement should show why you wish to study for a law degree. You can do this by providing answers to some of the following questions.

- Why do you wish to study law? Money, status or family traditions are not good reasons. Refer to evidence and the things that helped you reach your decision. For example: 'I am particularly interested in pursuing a career at the Bar. My enthusiasm was initially sparked by my active participation in the debating society at school, of which I am president. I found that I thoroughly enjoyed the challenge of putting across my point of view and trying to counteract the opposing argument.'
- What precisely is it about the law that interests you? Give details and examples, referring to recent cases and debates.
- Which particular area of law interests you most and, again, why?
- What related material have you recently read and why did you appreciate it (see below)?
- What legal cases have you followed and what recent judgments have you admired and why?
- What legal controversies have excited you?

Well-chosen references to books you have read, including specific information you have gleaned from them, are very helpful. Some suggested reading for aspiring law students is contained in Chapter 12. Be careful not to just reel off a list of books – be specific about what interested you about them and what you learnt from them. You should also refer to any law taster courses you have attended but, again, don't just mention them – spell out what you gained from going to them and how they helped you decide that you would like to study law. You should also refer to any current legal issues appearing in the press and what you think of them or have learnt from them.

Work experience is very useful as it demonstrates a commitment to the subject outside the classroom, so mention any experience, paid or voluntary. Explain concisely what your job entailed and what you got out of the whole experience. Even if you haven't been able to get work experience, if you have spoken to anyone in the legal profession about their job, then it is worth mentioning as it all builds up a picture of someone who is keen and has done some research. Wanting to be like the characters in legal dramas on television is not enough, and neither is wanting to follow in a parent's footsteps!

Future plans, if any, should also be included on your form. Do not mention a desire to make a lot of money, since this is unlikely to impress admissions tutors who may well have shunned lucrative career opportunities in order to pursue an academic career.

Why you are a good candidate

You should also set out what makes you a good candidate for a law degree. If you have already explained why you wish to be a lawyer and how you made that decision, you will already have gone a long way towards demonstrating that you will be a committed student of the law. However, you should also briefly explain how your current school subjects (usually A levels) prepare you for studying a law degree. What skills have they given you? If you have taken only maths and science A levels, you will need to describe how you are prepared for the more literary aspects of a law degree – i.e. reading and assimilating lots of information and preparing longer pieces of written work. You will need to show that you can write an essay.

Extra-curricular activities and transferrable skills

The last part of the statement should set out your extra-curricular activities, with a particular emphasis on what key transferable skills they have given you – for example, teamwork, self-motivation or leadership skills. If possible, you could try to link these in with the skills that will be necessary when studying for a law degree. If you are a school prefect, or team captain, then mention it here.

If you are planning to do so, state your reasons for applying for deferred entry and outline what you intend to do during your gap year. For example, you might be planning to find some relevant work experience in a firm of solicitors, and then spend some time overseas to brush up your language skills.

General advice

It is imperative that the focus of your personal statement is on the course of study that you wish to follow. Make sure that for each point you make, whether that be which A levels you are studying or the work experience that you have done, you are relating it back to the course.

Many universities now publish detailed advice about what they are looking for in a personal statement on their websites. You should carefully check the websites of the all the universities you wish to apply to and make sure that you follow their advice. Most of it will simply be along the lines of the advice given above, but you should make sure you address any specific requirements or suggestions from the universities you are particularly interested in. You should also bear in mind the way that the universities describe the courses you are interested in on their websites. For example, if they emphasise the need for a practical approach, then it makes sense to highlight how you demonstrate an ability to be practical.

Finally, you should try to avoid some common pitfalls when writing your statement.

- Avoid cheesy clichés (e.g. 'for as long as I can remember') and over-use of quotations. One short quotation is acceptable if it is relevant and you comment on it.
- Do not include unsupported statements (e.g. 'I am hard-working'), which lack credibility. Instead, give evidence to support statements (e.g. things you have done which proved your capacity for hard work).
- Do not refer to specific courses as the same statement will go to all five of your university choices. You will not be able to write a convincing statement if you are applying to a variety of different courses (see below).
- Do not lie or exaggerate. You must be prepared to be asked on anything you mention in your statement if you are called for interview.
- Do not try to be funny. Humour is very personal and can easily be misinterpreted or backfire.
- Do not be tempted to get someone else (a friend, teacher, parent or one of the many internet sites that offer 'help') to write your personal statement. It has to sound like you, which is why it is called a personal statement.

Caution!

- Never, ever, copy and paste any part of your statement from any other sources (whether from a friend or the examples in this book or somewhere online). UCAS runs all applications through anti-plagiarism software. If you do this, you will be caught out and your application will be void.

Make sure you print out a copy of your personal statement when you have finished it so that you can refer to it again and remind yourself what you said, should you be called for interview.

As emphasised in Chapter 1, it is not necessary to study law at university in order to become a lawyer (although it saves you a year of study). This chapter focuses on applying to university to study law, but if you are applying for a non-law degree, exactly the same issues arise. Your personal statement should focus on why you wish to study your particular subject at university and why you are a good candidate.

Warning: mixing courses and joint honours courses

You will write only one personal statement, which is read by admissions staff at the five courses for which you are applying, so you must make sure that it is suitable for all five courses. Each university sees only its name and course code on the form that UCAS sends to it: your other choices are not revealed. So, if you are applying to read psychology at one university (remember, you do not have to read law at university to become a lawyer), management at another, history at a third, and so on, then you cannot possibly write a personal statement that will satisfy the criteria for all of the courses. The psychology admissions tutor will wonder why you have written about history, and so on. The likelihood is that you will be rejected by all of your choices.

If you apply for a joint honours course such as law and French, your form will be seen by admissions tutors from both departments, each of whom will want to see that you are a serious candidate for his/her course. You must therefore cover both subjects in your statement.

Tips from admissions tutors

The following advice has all been given by law admissions tutors at leading university law schools over the last few years.

Admissions tutors want to see that you have a genuine reason for wanting to study law and have made your decision to apply for a law degree based on thorough research. You must show that you have thought carefully about why you want to study for a law degree and have properly researched the degree programmes you are applying for. Do not list your achievements without explaining their applicability to a law degree. You should also have an idea of the different areas of law you can work in, although it is perfectly acceptable not to have made up your mind yet about which area you would prefer.

You also need to show that you have a firm grasp of current affairs and regularly read a quality newspaper. An up-to-date understanding of the legal profession is also important. Some admissions tutors consider an awareness of current issues to be more important than reading law texts.

You should include any relevant work experience in your statement, although admissions tutors are very sensitive to the fact that not all students will have had the opportunity to get high-quality legal work experience. The general agenda to widen access to universities means that admissions tutors will make sure they avoid discriminating against applicants because of their background and the opportunities available to them. However, you still need to show what you have managed to do in the way of work experience and what you have learnt from it, even if it is not directly law related.

You should also:

- focus your personal statement on the course you are applying for
- make your personal statement sound like you
- apply early
- check carefully for spelling and grammatical errors.

Some sample personal statements for law degrees are shown below. Use these to get some ideas but **do not copy** any part of them into your own personal statement.

First sample personal statement *(3,847 characters)*

My interest in reading law at university originally stemmed from a school trip to the local magistrates' court, where we were allowed to participate in a mock trial. Before this, I had thought that the outcome of a trial was dependent only on the verbal skills of the defence or prosecuting lawyers: I had not realised how structured the process was, or how much control the judge has over proceedings. As a result of this, I joined the school's debating society, which has given me the confidence to present arguments in a structured and convincing way, which I believe is a vital skill for any lawyer. It has also allowed me to consolidate and expand my knowledge and understanding of current affairs because we often debate issues that are in the news, such as: 'Can military intervention in Syria, with its potential substantial loss of life, be justified on humanitarian grounds?'

To gain more insight into a legal career, I arranged work-shadowing with a local law firm (Brutal & Co) for two weeks. I was able to see how much paperwork was involved in preparing a case for trial and appreciate the importance of accuracy in all the documents involved. I was able to help with some of the cases that they were working on, including conveyancing and planning issues.

I then started to read about law and legal subjects in order to further my knowledge and understand what studying law involves. I began by reading *Understanding Law* by Adams and Brownsword, which contained a useful exploration of the English legal system. I also read *Glanville Williams: Learning the Law*, which was a very interesting introduction to studying law and really gave me the desire to study it further. I keep up to date with current political and legal issues by reading broadsheet newspapers and using the BBC News website. I have also recently read *Memoirs of a Radical Lawyer* by Michael Mansfield, which showed me that lawyers can have an effect on highlighting political as well as legal injustices.

I chose my A level subjects with a law degree in mind. Economics and history both require analytical skills, the ability to draw conclusions from documents, and to be able to argue the case for these conclusions. I enjoy the way that events can be interpreted in many different ways, and the need for careful assessment of 'evidence'. The global economic problems in 2007/2008 illustrated that even experts do not always get things right. French has been very useful, not only because it requires a good memory and the ability to learn material, but also because I have chosen to do my A2 coursework on the French legal system and how it differs from our system. I hope that I can work for an international law firm in the future, and so this research will be useful. In my Lower Sixth, I also studied art. Whilst this is not directly relevant to law, I believe that using my creative skills to take ideas and turn them into something new and exciting is a useful ability to have; and I also enjoy art very much.

Until the end of last year, I did a paper round before school every morning. While this clearly did not have any direct relevance to a legal career, it taught me the virtues of hard work and discipline: it was sometimes not easy to get up in the cold and dark and venture outside. In my spare time, I play the guitar in a jazz band with my friends. This allows me to relax and have fun, but we also have to make decisions as a group, so it has made me realise that it is important to listen to and respect other people's points of view and has helped me develop teamwork skills. I am also a school prefect this year, with special responsibility for planning teams for inter-house events, which has further developed my empathy and my leadership skills.

I am looking forward to studying law and believe I will be an industrious and enthusiastic student.

Second sample personal statement *(3,983 characters)*

I first became interested in the law after studying moral dilemmas. I was particularly interested in the case of cannibalism on the

Mignonette as discussed by Sandel in his lectures on justice. Adrift at sea, three sailors ate the cabin boy to survive. They were rescued but were then found guilty of murder. I wondered whether and how the law could allow for such extreme cases. Can laws be formulated with well-defined exceptions or are matters so complex that we have to proceed on a case-by-case basis? To further my knowledge, I read Hutchinson's *Is Eating People Wrong? Great Legal Cases and How They Shaped the World.* To develop my knowledge in general I read *The Law Machine* by Berlins and Dyer, which provided me with a solid grounding in the essential principles of the English legal system and highlighted its weaknesses. I also read *Letters to a Law Student* by McBride on what to expect in my first year of study.

My A level in philosophy has provided me with useful skills and knowledge for studying law. It has taught me how to analyse arguments and explore complex and abstract ideas. As well as studying different ethical theories and the difficulty of deciding whether the rightness of acts relates to their intrinsic nature or their consequences, I have enjoyed looking at the relationship between the mind and the brain. Chemical changes in the brain affect our capacity to reason and act. I was intrigued by whether our genes and our upbringing could also affect our capacity for self-control. If so, then can people be responsible for their actions or will there be inevitable consequences of formative factors? It was interesting to speculate on what a legal system would be like if we could only rarely say that acts were freely chosen.

Studying government and politics has given me an understanding of the political ideologies that shape the British constitution and influence government policy. English literature has helped me to develop analytical skills and to assess the significance of language. This will be most advantageous in studying law, as a single word can change context and meaning completely, for example when looking at statutory interpretation.

I am fortunate in having had two work experience placements. I shadowed a barrister and witnessed the everyday duties he had at first hand. I watched him preparing for cases in his chambers and visiting the Crown Court daily, meeting defendants and observing cases. I found the proceedings fascinating. One case in particular stays with me, where a man was tried for physically abusing his wife. Even though the allegations were terrible, it made me realise the importance of the presumption of innocence and the right to a fair trial. It further highlighted the importance of the 'cab-rank rule' in ensuring fairness.

I have also experienced life as a solicitor at Statler and Waldorf. I worked in many departments including: Employment, Family and Divorce, Personal Injury, Clinical Negligence and Probate. I found my work in Clinical Negligence to be extremely interesting as I had not appreciated its importance and had been put off by the many 'make-a-claim' advertisements on television. In one case, a man had received a kidney from a donor with cancer that resulted in him contracting cancer too. It made me realise that there are many people who do deserve compensation due to negligence. Both placements deepened my desire to study law, but the latter placement inspired me to study to be a solicitor.

At school, I am a keen participant in the debating society, which has helped me learn to put together a convincing argument. Now that I am in my final year I am also a mentor to younger students, which has taught me a lot about communication and leadership. I play rugby and squash regularly and enjoy hiking. I am a mature, hard-working individual who is determined to face the challenges of a law degree, and I hope to contribute a lot, educationally and socially, to the university.

Third sample personal statement *(3,954 characters)*

Since my first visit to the public gallery of the law courts, I have been fascinated by the criminal system. On trial was a man accused of raping a young woman at a party, in a far from clear-cut case, which was argued eloquently by my friend's father, the defence QC. The QC's silver tongue and charm, in my opinion, did as many favours to the defendant as the facts themselves, and I saw there the true skill of an advocate and of an immensely sharp mind. It led me to participate in the Bar National Mock Trial competition, reaching the national final in my AS year, arguing for the defence a case of racism within the police. What I enjoyed most was understanding and acting each of the roles within the courtroom during the competition.

I was moved to read Trevor Grove's books *The Juryman's Tale* and *The Magistrate's Tale* which both gave a practical insight into these lay positions within the legal system. I found it difficult to comprehend the amount of trust put into the hands of these lay people, magistrates in particular, but, on reflection, I fundamentally agree with Lord Denning that they are 'the lamp that shows that freedom lives' and sincerely hope that we continue to develop our respect for them (unlike the days when they were locked away without food or water for arriving at the 'wrong' verdict). A system that leaves crucial decisions to a small number of 'ordinary', unpaid and even prejudiced people will always be open to question. However, it can equally be seen as a system that allows for society's involvement in justice and protection of the justice system from the state.

Working in a medical negligence solicitor's practice over the summer gave me a different insight into the law and legal system in this country. There has been a rise in clinical negligence cases in recent times as patients and their families seek compensation for poor treatment. While often there are legal grounds for these cases, I was struck by the way many of them are mainly driven by the emotions of the relatives involved. Equally, it is putting a lot of strain on the medical profession in an age when doctors are now publically reviewed. I learnt the fundamentals of teamwork while undertaking due diligence work on a case involving the retention of organs post-mortem, a common theme nowadays. I also understood that in order to succeed in medical negligence claims, it was necessary to prove facts 'on the balance of probability' rather than beyond reasonable doubt. It made me realise that our legal system has so many variables that often change depending on the area of law; it is one of the principal reasons for me wishing to study this course.

I believe my A level choices have prepared me well to study for a law degree. History has allowed me to develop my essay writing skills and required me to read and understand a lot of factual information. Economics has given me a greater understanding of current affairs, which is crucial for a lawyer, and, finally, studying A level Maths has sharpened my ability to think clearly and logically, which again is very important for a lawyer.

Outside of my studies, I believe in keeping busy and enjoy playing sport. I am captain of the lacrosse team and enjoy the team-based camaraderie that comes with it. While playing lacrosse has developed my team working skills, being captain has helped me develop leadership skills, which should both be useful in a legal career. I also completed my Gold Duke of Edinburgh Award this year and learnt a great deal from the different challenges it presented. I think my biggest lesson was gaining the tenacity and resilience required to complete it; two skills that will be invaluable in the legal profession.

Sometimes, things are not always as they seem. Often you have to look beyond the obvious to find the truth. This is why law fascinates me and this is why I wish to forge a career in a profession that demands as much from me as I do from it.

The LNAT

The LNAT is the National Admissions Test for Law. It is an externally set test which is used by a number of universities to help them select suitable candidates either for interview or for conditional offers. It does not test legal knowledge, but instead tests your aptitude for the skills required to study law, in particular:

- verbal reasoning
- ability to understand and interpret information
- ability to analyse information and draw conclusions
- deductive and inductive reasoning abilities.

The test lasts two-and-a-quarter hours and is in two sections – a multiple-choice section and an essay.

The multiple-choice section (95 minutes) is computer based and consists of 42 questions, based on passages of text setting out fictional scenarios. The score for this section is known as your LNAT score.

The essay section (40 minutes) tests your ability to construct logical, structured and clear arguments by writing one essay chosen from a list of essay questions. The essay is not actually marked by LNAT but is passed on to the participating universities with your LNAT score.

The best way to prepare yourself for the LNAT is to do several practice tests. The LNAT website (www.lnat.ac.uk) contains further details and also plenty of specimen questions and practice papers. There is also a practice test simulator that you can download. This is an on-screen simulation of the LNAT and includes a tutorial and two live practice tests. These will allow you to familiarise yourself with the format of the test and the skills it requires.

Because the multiple-choice section is based on fairly substantial passages of text, it is not really practical to reproduce one here as an example. You should therefore go to the LNAT website and look at these. However, some examples of the sort of essay questions you may be asked are:

1. In what circumstances should abortion be permitted and why?
2. Would you agree that travel and tourism exploit poorer nations and benefit only the richer ones?
3. Wearing a burkha in Western countries is just as offensive as wearing a bikini in Arab countries. Do you agree?

Many more examples are available on the LNAT website.

The LNAT is used by the following universities at the time of writing:

- Birmingham
- Bristol

- Durham
- Glasgow
- King's College London
- Nottingham
- Oxford
- SOAS
- University College London.

(See below for details about the University of Cambridge)

The deadline for registering and booking the LNAT is normally 15 January, and the test must be sat by 20 January (5 October and 20 October, respectively, for the University of Oxford), but check the LNAT website for details (www.lnat. ac.uk).

- To sit the LNAT, you must register on the LNAT website. Registration usually opens in August in the year before entry and testing usually starts in September. The test is sat at an external test centre.
- The cost of the test (for 2016 entry) is £50 at UK and EU test centres, and £70 for other centres. The fee is payable online by credit or debit card at the time of booking.
- You can sit the test only once in any application cycle. If you sit it a second time, the later result will not count.
- If you reapply to universities that require the LNAT in subsequent years, you will have to sit the LNAT again.
- Information for candidates who may need extra time (for example, students with dyslexia) or need special arrangements (for example, students with sight or mobility problems) can be found on the LNAT website.

For more help on the LNAT admissions tests read *Practise & Pass Professional: LNAT* (Trotman, 2011).

University of Cambridge

The University of Cambridge stopped using the LNAT test in 2010. It has replaced it with the Cambridge Law Test, which is used by nearly all Cambridge colleges. It consists of a one-hour paper that is normally sat when you attend for your interview. Details can be found on the University of Cambridge website (www.law.cam.ac.uk).

8 | Succeeding at interview

Outside Oxford and Cambridge, formal interviews are rarely part of the admissions process for law degrees. Most universities, even those in the highly respected Russell Group of top universities, do not interview candidates for law degrees at all, other than those with unusual qualifications or mature students, in which cases, the universities interview because they need more information to help them make a decision. Interviews are expensive and time consuming for both the university and the applicants. One notable exception at the time of writing is the University of York Law School, which does interview applicants. Oxford and Cambridge also interview all applicants. If you are invited to attend an academic interview, this chapter contains some guidance on what to expect at the interview and how to prepare for it.

You may also be invited to an interview for work experience at a firm of solicitors or set of barristers' chambers. Much of the advice in this chapter is equally relevant to this situation and the same recommendations also apply. A few additional tips that apply particularly to interviews for work experience are given at the end of the chapter.

Oxbridge and York examples

Guides to interviews, including sample questions, and even video examples, are available on the websites of the universities of Oxford, Cambridge and York.

- www.ox.ac.uk/admissions/undergraduate/applying-to-oxford/interviews/interview-timetable?
- www.ox.ac.uk/admissions/undergraduate/applying-to-oxford/interviews/sample-interview-questions
- www.undergraduate.study.cam.ac.uk/applying/interviews
- www.york.ac.uk/law/undergraduate/interview

What to expect at the interview

The purpose of an interview is to test your:

- motivation to study law

- logical reasoning ability
- effective communication skills.

The university is not seeking to test your prior knowledge of the law.

You are likely to be asked questions on the following:

- why you wish to study law
- why you wish to go to that particular university
- your academic qualifications
- the personal statement in your UCAS form
- some questions on legal issues which are designed to assess your logical reasoning and communication skills.

You will also be asked whether there is anything you would like to ask your interviewer.

Interviews need not be daunting. They are designed to help those asking the questions to find out as much about you as they can. Interviewers are more interested in what you know than in what you do not.

The interview is a chance for you to demonstrate your knowledge of, commitment to and enthusiasm for the law. Interviewers clearly wish to know your reasons for wanting to study law and, possibly above all, they will be looking to see whether you have a mind capable of developing logical arguments and the ability to articulate such arguments powerfully and coherently. You should view an interview as a chance to put yourself across well rather than as an obstacle course designed to catch you out.

Preparation for a law interview

Once you have been asked to attend an interview, it is sensible to prepare thoroughly. You should take the time to think through your answers to some of the questions you are likely to be asked. You should also be very well informed about the course you are applying for and any current legal issues which you might be asked about. Try to arrange some mock interviews, carried out by a teacher at school, careers adviser, family friend, or anyone else you can persuade to help. These can be very useful. Reeling off pre-prepared answers to questions is obviously not going to impress an interviewer, but thinking in advance about what you are likely to be asked about can help you get your thoughts in order and sound confident and prepared at the interview.

Re-read your personal statement

You are very likely to be asked questions about your personal state-ment, so read it through well before the interview and make sure you can remember and speak coherently about any books you mentioned having read. If you have followed the advice contained in Chapter 7 of this book, you will not have included anything in your statement that you are not prepared to speak about at interview. Take a copy of the statement with you to the interview and read it through again shortly beforehand.

Make sure you know all about the course and the university

Read through all the information on the university's website relevant to the course you have chosen and also read any brochures or other written information you may have been given at any open day you attended.

Practise getting the right body language

This is not as obvious as it seems, so a small amount of practice will make all the difference. Use mock interviews to give you some practice of walking into a room, looking your interviewer in the eyes, smiling, saying hello and shaking their hand. The handshake should be firm and confident – but without crushing their fingers. Sit down upright in your seat and do not slouch or lean back too far. You want to look interested and engaged and also relaxed, but not overly casual.

Be informed about current affairs

It is important to keep up to date with current affairs by reading a quality daily newspaper. It is particularly important to be aware of any current legal issues being discussed in the press, as these present an obvious topic on which you can be asked questions. Ethical issues, political issues, police issues, prison reform issues – all of these are possible topics for questions at interview.

The quality broadsheet newspapers (such as the *Independent*, *The Times* and the *Guardian*) all include reports on current legal issues. You could also read *The Law Society Gazette* or *The Lawyer*, which are published weekly in print format and are also available online. *The Law Society Gazette* contains reviews of current legal issues and matters affecting the legal profession. *The Lawyer* tends to focus more on news and comment about comings and goings in the legal profession (such as mergers between law firms). Following the law reports in the press will give you further insight into any important current legal cases. You may well be asked if you have read about any cases recently.

Listening to certain quality radio programmes and watching current affairs television programmes can also be helpful. Many current issues discussed on radio and television have legal implications. Television's *Question Time*, *Newsnight* and certain *Panorama*-style documentaries and Radio 4's *Today* programme, *The World This Weekend* and *Today in Parliament* are all examples of potentially useful programmes to help you build up a thorough knowledge of current affairs. You could also visit the legal websites mentioned in the 'Further information' chapter at the end of the book.

Recent events are very likely to form a part of the interview. What do you think should be happening in the prison system at the moment?

What reforms would you like to see implemented in the running of the police force?

Don't forget that interview skills are greatly improved by practice. Chat through the sorts of issues mentioned above with your friends or family and then practise discussing them at mock interviews you have arranged.

Why do you wish to study law?

This is an obvious question and you should think about your reasons carefully before the interview. Reasons for wishing to study law vary. A passion for television courtroom drama series is not enough. You need to think about the everyday practice of the law in this country and it is very useful to spend time talking with lawyers of all kinds and learning from them what is involved. You may well be asked whether you have spoken to any lawyers about their work or visited any courts.

It is important to be aware of the many types of law that lawyers practise – criminal, contract, family, taxation, etc. – and be clear about the differences between them. You may be asked what areas of law you are particularly interested in or whether you hope to become a barrister or solicitor (although you would not be expected to have come to any firm decisions at this stage). You should be clear in your mind about the difference between them.

Joint degree subjects

If you have chosen a joint or combined honours course, then obviously you will have to prepare yourself for questions on the other subject you are hoping to study alongside law as well as questions on law.

Questions on legal issues

Knowledge of the structure of the legal and judicial systems is vital. Read Chapter 2 of this book to give you a basic understanding of the legal system. You should know who the Lord Chief Justice is, who the Director of Public Prosecutions is and what he or she does. You should be aware of recent controversial legal decisions, who took them and what their consequences are or could be. Who is the Home Secretary and why is he or she important?

Interviewers will ask questions with a view to being in a position to form an opinion about the quality of your thought and your ability to argue a particular case. You may be presented with a real or supposed set of circumstances and then be asked to comment on the legal implications of them. Is euthanasia wrong? What is the purpose of prison?

At the end of this chapter there are some sample questions, which show the type of legal questions you may be asked. Questions may be straightforward and specific, but can also involve more convoluted scenarios for you to think through. Remember that there are no right or wrong answers – you simply need to show that you can think through the issues in a logical and reasoned way and communicate your arguments and conclusions effectively.

On the day: practicalities and general advice

Arrive early

Make sure you know where you are going and leave plenty of time to get there. Allow for trains and buses to be delayed. Print off a map before you leave home and make sure you take the telephone number of the admissions office so that if, despite your best efforts, you are still late, you can phone and let them know. Remember to re-read your personal statement just before the interview.

Dress carefully

Dress comfortably, but show that you are taking the interview seriously: wear smart, clean clothes. Do not wear anything too revealing. You should also clean your shoes and make sure your hair is neat.

Be calm

Take a few deep breaths before the interview and, if you are nervous, try to calm and relax yourself. Listen to a favourite piece of music or something that you know will make you feel more relaxed. Remember you wouldn't have been invited for interview unless you were a serious candidate for a place, so be confident and let your talents shine through!

Demeanour during the interview

- Be yourself.
- Be enthusiastic and show a strong commitment to your subject.
- Maintain good eye contact with your interviewer(s) and confident body language.
- Listen carefully to the questions you are asked and make sure you understand what you are being asked before you answer. Don't be afraid to ask questions if you are unsure of what the interviewer wants.
- Be concise and logical – put forward your answer and use examples and factual knowledge to reinforce your points.
- If you are asked a question you don't know the answer to, say so. To waffle simply wastes time and lets you down. To lie, of course, is even worse – especially for aspiring lawyers!
- Be willing to consider new ideas, if your interview involves discussion of legal or other current issues. An ability to see the opposite point of view while maintaining your own will mark you out as strong law degree material.
- Show a willingness to learn and be prepared to admit defeat if you put forward an argument that is demolished by your interviewer. A touch of humility will not hurt.

An ability to think on your feet is vital – another prerequisite for a good lawyer. Although you will (hopefully) have thought through answers to some of the questions you are likely to be asked, you do not want to sound as though you are reeling off a pre-learned answer as this will sound false and will not impress anyone.

Much of the practice of law in this country rests on an adversarial system, so don't be surprised if you receive an adversarial interview.

Remember to keep calm and think clearly!

Think of some questions to ask your interviewer(s)

At the end of the interview, you will almost certainly be given the chance to ask if you have any questions. It is sensible to have one or two questions of a serious kind – to do with the course, the tuition and so on – up your sleeve. It is not wise, obviously, to ask them anything that you could and should have found out from the prospectus. If there is nothing, then say that your interview has covered all that you had thought of.

Above all, end on a positive note and remember to smile!

The interview for work experience

Most of the advice in this chapter will equally apply if you are going for an interview for work experience to a firm of solicitors or a set of chambers. However, in addition you should do the following.

- Research the firm/chambers thoroughly before interview. Look at their brochure and website.
- Plan in advance what you think your key selling points are to the employer and make sure you find an opportunity in the interview to get your points across.
- Prepare a few questions about the firm to ask your interviewer at the end. You can demonstrate your preparation here by asking them about something you have read about the firm/chambers recently, if appropriate.
- Dress smartly and appropriately. Lawyers tend to look quite formal, so a suit is probably appropriate in this situation.

Sample interview questions on legal issues

Here are a few sample legal questions which show the type of thing you may be asked.

1. Should cannabis/euthanasia be legalised?
2. What are the pros and cons of fusing the two branches of the legal profession?

3. Should the police in this country be armed?
4. If you were in a position of power, would you change the current civil legal aid situation?
5. Should the police spend their time enforcing the laws concerned with begging?
6. What do you think of recent law reforms?
7. What are your views on the right to silence?
8. How can you quantify compensation for victims of crime?
9. Should criminals be allowed to sell their stories as 'exclusives'?
10. Is it 'barbaric' to cane someone for vandalising cars?
11. How does the law affect your daily life?
12. What would happen if there were no law?
13. Is it necessary for the law to be entrenched in archaic tradition, ritual and jargon?
14. How are law and morality related?
15. Do you believe that all people have equal access to justice?
16. What is justice?
17. Why do we send criminals to prison? What are the alternatives?
18. Should the media be more careful with the way in which they report real crime?
19. Do you think the press should be allowed to report the names of celebrities when unproven allegations of sexual abuse have been made against them?
20. Is law the best way to handle situations such as domestic violence/ child abuse/rape?
21. What causes crime rates to increase?
22. Is trial by jury a good idea? Should anyone be allowed to serve on a jury?
23. Do you think capital punishment should be reinstated?
24. Should the law permit suspected terrorists to be held indefinitely without trial?
25. If shop-lifting were punishable by death, and therefore nobody did it, would that be a just and effective law?
26. You are driving along a busy road with the window down when a swarm of bees flies into your car. You panic and lose control of the car, causing a huge pile-up. Are you legally responsible?
27. A blind person, travelling by train, gets out at his/her destination. Unfortunately the platform is shorter than the train, and the blind person falls to the ground, sustaining several injuries. Who, if anyone, should compensate him/her?
28. A cyclist rides the wrong way down a one-way street and a chimney falls on him. What legal proceedings should he take? What if he is riding down a private drive signed 'no trespassing'?

9 | Non-standard applications

Not everyone decides that they want to be a lawyer at an early age. Many successful lawyers are people who started out down a completely different career path. Equally, a number of successful lawyers in the UK come from overseas. Law firms and chambers welcome applicants from a wide range of backgrounds, and often have diversity initiatives in place. This chapter offers a brief overview of non-standard applications. For more information, please check with individual universities or the professional representative bodies for solicitors and barristers – i.e. the Law Societies of England and Wales, Scotland and Northern Ireland or, for aspiring barristers, the Bar Council of England and Wales, the Faculty of Advocates in Scotland or the Bar of Northern Ireland. Website addresses for all these institutions are given in Chapter 12.

Graduates with degrees other than law

Many lawyers, particularly in England and Wales, have obtained a degree in a subject other than law. As is explained more fully in the relevant sections of Chapter 4, this simply necessitates taking a further postgraduate qualification in law in order to cover the material that would usually be studied during a law degree. This qualification is the GDL in England and Wales, a two-year accelerated law degree in Scotland and a Masters in Law in Northern Ireland. The additional qualification is taken before moving on to the vocational stage of training. Please see the relevant sections of Chapter 4 for more information. Many employers positively welcome applications from non-law graduates, with the different range of skills that they bring. There are, however, financial implications as an extra year (two in Scotland) of study will need to be funded.

Mature students

Many law firms and sets of chambers positively welcome new recruits who are embarking on law as a second career. Experience or knowledge of particular business or industry sectors which form a law firm's client base can be especially welcomed. For example, former medical practitioners have the knowledge and experience to become excellent medical negligence lawyers. Many lawyers have not gone straight from school and university to the legal profession.

The possible routes for mature students to enter the legal professions depends on their level of academic qualifications.

Mature students who have a degree in a subject other than law are in the same position as other non-law graduates (discussed above) and are eligible to apply for the GDL or its equivalent outside England and Wales.

Mature students who do not have a degree can, if they can satisfy the entry requirements (i.e. they have A level or equivalent qualifications) simply apply to university as a mature student to obtain the necessary degree. If you are in this situation, it would make sense to make sure that your chosen degree is a Qualifying Law Degree (see Chapter 4, page 42 for more details) to ensure that it will satisfy the academic stage of legal training and allow you to move straight on to the vocational stage of training (which is also summarised in Chapter 4).

Mature students without A levels (or equivalent qualifications) would need to take an Access to Higher Education course at a local further education college before applying to university. Each year around 20,000 Access to HE students apply for a degree course at a UK university to study subjects including law. These courses are outlined on page 41 in the section in Chapter 4 relating to England and Wales. In Scotland, a different system, called the Scottish Wider Access Programme, operates and Northern Irish universities have their own arrangements for access courses. More details are available at www.accesstohe.ac.uk.

Alternatively, there are non-graduate routes to becoming a lawyer and these are also outlined in the relevant sections of Chapter 4. For example, the solicitors' profession in England and Wales offers a number of non-graduate entry routes, which are summarised in Figure 1 on page 39 and then explained more fully on page 44. Non-graduate routes to qualifying are also available in Scotland (see page 51) and Northern Ireland (page 52).

Overseas students

Overseas students who already have a degree in their own country may apply to either the Solicitors Regulation Authority (for aspiring solicitors) or the Bar Standards Board (for barristers) for a certificate of academic standing, which will then allow them to take the GDL in England and Wales, in the same way as non-law graduates (see above).

Alternatively, overseas students might wish to start their training to become a UK lawyer by applying to study for their degree at a UK university. If you are in this situation, then the advice and guidance contained in Chapters 6 and 7 applies equally to you. However, the statistics show that overseas students are quite a lot less successful than UK students in gaining places at UK universities to read law, as the Law Society's figures for 2014 entry show:

Applicants' nationality	Number of applicants	Places	% Success
UK	23,030	16,980	74%
Overseas	8,770	4,795	55%

Table 4: Nationality and success rate for university law degree courses

This section therefore includes particular advice for overseas applicants on applying to a UK university to read law.

The process of applying as an international student is similar to that used by UK students: you use the same online UCAS form, provide the same information, and have the same deadlines. The differences are likely to be these:

● The examinations you have taken and/or will be taking may not appear in the drop-down menus on the UCAS form.
● The fee codes and support arrangements will be different.
● Your school may not have registered with UCAS and so you may have to apply as a private individual rather than through an institution.

Detailed advice about how to fill in the UCAS form, and to deal with these issues, can be found in the 'Apply' section of the UCAS website (www.ucas.com). This section of the UCAS website contains special advice for international students for each section of the UCAS form. There is also a summary of tips for international students (www.ucas.com/ucas/undergraduate/getting-started/international-and-eu-students/tips-international-applications).

However, many well-qualified, serious and motivated international students are unsuccessful in their applications because they or their referees (or both) are unfamiliar with what the university selectors are looking for in two particular sections of the application form:

1. the personal statement
2. the reference.

The personal statement

Students who have applied for universities outside of the UK may be familiar with the idea of writing a statement about themselves to support their applications. These can often take the form of a 'hard sell', in which the student extols his or her personal qualities, achievements, hopes and dreams. This format is not suitable for a UCAS personal statement, which needs to focus on the course itself, and what the student has done to investigate it. The advice given in Chapter 7 is equally applicable to international students, and you should read it carefully. The UCAS website also recommends that you should specifically mention in your personal statement why you want to study in the UK, your English language skills (and any tests or courses you have taken) and why you do not want to study in your own country.

The reference

Often, a promising application is rejected because the person providing the reference is unfamiliar with what is required, and the selectors have no choice other than to reject because they are not given enough information. UCAS references need to focus on the following:

- the student's suitability for the course and level of study
- an assessment of the student's academic performance to date (including the student's level of English if this is not his or her first language)
- how the student will adapt to studying in the UK
- the student's personal qualities.

If you are unsure as to whether the person who will write your reference fully understands what is required, show them the section on the UCAS website called 'How to write UCAS undergraduate references': www.ucas.com/advisers/references/how-write-ucas-undergraduate-references.

LNAT

Some universities require candidates to sit the Law National Admissions Test (LNAT) in addition to gaining academic qualifications. This online test can be sat outside of the UK. See Chapter 7, pages 89–90 for more details.

Academic qualifications

The UCAS website (www.ucas.com) gives details of the acceptable non-UK qualifications. The international sections on individual university websites will provide further details. International students whose local qualifications are not acceptable to UK universities will need to study A levels or the equivalent either at an international school in their own country or at a school or college in the UK, or possibly follow a one-year university Foundation course. Details of providers of UK qualifications can be found on the British Council website (www.educationuk.org/global/articles/further-education-institutions).

10| Results day

A level results day is arguably one of the most important days of your life, but don't panic: this chapter will provide you with some calm and practical advice on what to do on the day, whatever your results are.

The A level results will arrive at your school on the third Thursday in August. The universities will have received them a few days earlier. It is much better for you to go into school in person on the day the results are published, so do not arrange to be away on holiday then. Do not wait for the results slip to be posted to you. Try to get hold of your results as soon as possible on the day, because if you need to act to secure your place or go through Clearing, then time is of the essence because you will be competing with other students in the same situation. If you live overseas and are unable to go into school, make sure that you get hold of your results in some other way as soon as possible on results day.

Hopefully, you will need to do nothing other than celebrate! If you have a conditional offer and your grades equal or exceed that offer, then you can relax and wait for your chosen university to send you joining instructions. To check that all is in order, you can log on to the 'Track' facility on the UCAS website to make sure that your place has been confirmed.

> **Tip!**
>
> One word of warning: you cannot assume that equivalent grades such as A*AB will satisfy an AAA offer. Always check with your chosen university.

If your results are not as good as you had expected, or better than you expected, or you did not receive an offer from any of your chosen universities, then there are a number of options.

What to do if your grades are significantly better than anticipated

You may have significantly beaten the terms of your firm offer and now think that you might like to go somewhere 'better'. UCAS now uses a scheme called Adjustment, which is aimed at applicants who achieved better grades than predicted. It is primarily designed for students who might have been predicted low grades and therefore applied to universities that would accept them rather than where they really wanted to go. The Adjustment system allows you to put your existing firm offer on hold for a short period of time (five days) while contacting other universities where the standard offers are higher to see whether they will offer you a place with your higher grades. If you do not secure a new offer within this time period, or if you do not like what else is available, your original firm offer still stands and can still be accepted. Full details can be found on the UCAS website.

Alternatively, you may choose to withdraw from UCAS and reapply the following year with your higher grades.

What to do if you hold an offer but miss the grades

If you have only narrowly missed the required grades (either for your 'firm' or 'insurance' choice) it is important that you and your referee contact the university as soon as possible on results day, because you may be able to persuade the university still to accept you.

If you miss the grades for your firm choice, but meet the grades for your insurance choice, you will automatically be accepted onto the insurance place. You can still contact your first choice institution to see whether or not it will accept you.

If you do not achieve the grades required for either your firm or insurance choice, and you are unable to persuade either university still to accept you, then you are eligible to enter Clearing. This is a list of places that are still available on various courses at all of the universities. The list is published in national newspapers and on the UCAS website. Places on law degrees available through Clearing will be few and far between, but if there is a place available at a university you would be interested in going to, then you must contact the university by telephone as quickly as possible on results day, because you will be competing with other students in the same position. Clearing is a stressful system and you must make your decisions carefully and in a measured way despite the time pressure. There is no point in accepting a place at a university you do not genuinely want to go to.

In reality, due to the popularity of law as a degree, you should not pin your hopes on obtaining an offer of a place through Clearing. You may find that despite your best efforts, there simply are not any places available on law courses at universities where you would want to study. If you are unable to obtain a suitable place through Clearing, your best option would be to withdraw from UCAS altogether and then wait and reapply in the next academic year to courses for which you meet the entry requirements, with the benefit of your A level results to support your application. Given what has been said about the importance of choosing your university law course in Chapter 6, you do not want to settle for any university just because it has a place available, but hold out for a place at a university you are actually really enthusiastic about going to. In the meantime, you can use the time constructively by getting some work experience to build up your CV. You may also want to consider retaking some or all of your A levels in order to improve your chances of getting into a university you are really interested in going to.

What to do if you have no offer

If all of the universities that you applied to rejected you, you may have managed to find an offer through UCAS Extra. This scheme allows you to apply to other universities, either for law or for other courses. You will automatically be sent details by UCAS. UCAS Extra starts in February. If UCAS Extra does not provide you with an offer, you can enter Clearing in August once you have your results – see the details on Clearing above.

However, if you did not receive any offers when you applied, perhaps because your AS results were not particularly strong, but you have ended up with better A level results than expected, then you need to make universities aware of this. Try to get in touch with them as early as possible on results day to see if they will reconsider their decision in the light of your results. The best way to do this is by telephone and e-mail, and your UCAS referee may be able to help you in this respect. Try to persuade your referee to ring the admissions officers on your behalf – they will find it easier to get through than you will – or to e-mail a note in support of your application.

Retaking your A levels

This may be a sensible option for students who know they are capable of achieving better grades than they did first time round. However, you should be aware that the grade requirements for retake candidates are often higher than for first-timers. You should investigate the particular universities you are interested in to find out what they require from retake students. Also remember that, since September 2013, January A level exams and resits have been abolished, so if you are going to retake then it will have to be in the following summer session.

Independent sixth-form colleges provide specialist advice and teaching for students considering A level retakes. Interviews to discuss this are free and carry no obligation to enrol on a course, so it is worth taking the time to talk to their staff before you make any final decisions. Many will be able to give advice on results day if necessary.

Extenuating circumstances

If your grades were below those that were predicted or expected because of extenuating circumstances such as illness or family problems during exam time, make sure that you have written confirmation of this (such as a letter from a doctor, solicitor or someone at your school or college) and send this to the admissions department for your chosen course. The extenuating circumstances should be serious enough to merit special consideration and not just minor irritations.

Ideally, if something does go wrong at the time you are sitting your exams, you or your school/college should inform the universities immediately, warning them that you might not achieve the grades. It is more likely that they can make concessions then rather than when they have already made decisions about who to accept when the results are issued.

11 | Fees and funding

Seeking to qualify as a lawyer is expensive: first (usually) you have to fund a university degree and then you need to fund the vocational stage of training (possibly preceded by a postgraduate qualification in law, such as the GDL in England and Wales, if your degree was not in law). This chapter looks at the fees for the university degree stage of qualification and how those fees are funded. The fees and funding arrangements for postgraduate studies in law and the vocational stage of training depend on whether you wish to qualify as a solicitor or barrister, the qualification route you choose, and which jurisdiction within the UK you live in. The fees and funding arrangements for these courses are therefore discussed in Chapter 4 under the relevant headings for the different qualifications.

With respect to degree funding, most UK students are now accustomed to the idea of paying tuition fees to go to university, following their initial introduction in England in 1998 and subsequent significant increases in 2006 and 2012. This chapter briefly outlines the current fee structure for UK universities and the way in which the governments of the constituent countries of the UK help students fund their university studies. More information can be found at www.gov.uk/student-finance.

UK students

Universities in the UK can charge students up to £9,000 a year in tuition fees, and most of the higher-ranked universities in England now charge the maximum amount. Private colleges and universities are not subject to the £9,000 maximum, so can charge more. In most cases, these fees are not actually charged directly to students as the vast majority of students take out a student loan, which is repayable only after graduation and only once certain salary thresholds are reached (see below).

Rather confusingly, there are different fee structures and different types and levels of financial assistance available, depending on which part of the UK you are from and where you choose to study. These are very briefly summarised below, but you should check the websites of individual universities to find out how much that university is intending to charge and also visit the recommended government websites below for more information about student finance.

English residents

English students will pay tuition fees of up to £9,000 wherever they study in the UK. A tuition fee loan is available to cover the whole of these fees.

As well as tuition fee loans, maintenance loans are also available to cover your living expenses while you are at university. There used to be maintenance grants available for students from lower-income households, but these have now been scrapped and for students beginning their courses in September 2016 or later, all money available for living expenses now comes in the form of a student loan. The amount of maintenance loan is income-assessed. The guaranteed portion of the loan (which is less than half) is available to all students, but those from lower-income households are able to borrow higher amounts on a sliding scale up to the maximum loan available (which is £8,200 for outside London and £10,702 for London for 2016/2017).

The tuition fee loan and the maintenance loan are repayable via the income tax system only after you have graduated and only if and when you are earning more than £21,000. The repayments are a fixed part of your income and therefore depend on your future earnings and not on the size of your loan. All remaining debt is wiped after 30 years if it has not been fully repaid by then. Many commentators have described the loans as more akin to a graduate tax than a loan in the true sense of the word.

Applications for a student loan are made through the Government's Student Finance website at www.gov.uk/apply-for-student-finance. You can not apply for student finance for the 2016/2017 academic year until 2016. The deadline for applying is nine months after the start of the academic year.

Welsh residents

Welsh students will also be charged up to £9,000 wherever they study in the UK. However, regardless of where in the UK they study, they are entitled to a fee grant from the Welsh Government of up to £5,190 a year (for 2015 starters) towards their tuition fees. The first £3,810 of their tuition fees will be funded by a tuition fee loan and the grant will then cover the difference between the loan and the amount charged by the student's university.

The rules for living expenses and maintenance loans also differ from those in England. For more information on fees and student finance available in Wales please visit the following website: www.studentfinancewales.co.uk.

Northern Ireland residents

Northern Irish students will pay up to £9,000 per year tuition fees if they study in England, Wales or Scotland, but will pay a reduced fee (£3,805 for 2015 starters) if they study in Northern Ireland. For more information on fees and student finance available in Northern Ireland please visit the following website: www.studentfinanceni.co.uk.

Scottish residents

Scottish students will not pay any tuition fees if they go to a Scottish university, but they will pay up to £9,000 if they study anywhere else in the UK. Again, there are different rules for help with funding living expenses and there are some living-costs grants available for students from lower-income households. For more information on fees and student finance available in Scotland please visit the website of the Student Awards Agency Scotland: www.saas.gov.uk.

EU students

Students from other EU countries will be charged up to £9,000 if they study in England, Wales or Northern Ireland, but will not pay fees if they study in Scotland. For more information about tuition fees and student finance available for EU students please visit the relevant government websites (listed above) as well as the finance pages on individual university websites.

Non-EU international students

The fees for non-EU students do not have an upper limit and will depend on the course and the university. International students should contact individual universities for information on the fees they will be charging non-EU students. For more information please visit the website of the UK Council for International Student Affairs, which also has advice on student visa applications: www.ukcisa.org.uk.

Bursaries and scholarships

UK universities now offer a wide range of bursaries and scholarships to support some of their students. In order to charge the maximum permitted tuition fees of £9,000, universities must prove that they are awarding bursaries to poorer students. These are contributions towards the cost of going to university that do not have to be repaid. The terms of these will vary between the universities and you should check the universities' websites carefully to see whether you may be able to apply for any financial help. Usually, bursaries are completely dependent on your household income, whereas scholarships are at least partly dependent on academic or extra-curricular (e.g. sporting) ability.

12| Further information

Useful websites

Legal professions

Solicitors

The Law Society (of England and Wales)
www.lawsociety.org.uk
   Statistics:
   www.lawsociety.org.uk/policy-campaigns/research-trends/annual-
   statistical-reports/

Solicitors Regulation Authority
www.sra.org.uk

The Law Society of Scotland
www.lawscot.org.uk

The Law Society of Northern Ireland
www.lawsoc-ni.org

Barristers

The Bar Council of England and Wales
www.barcouncil.org.uk

The Bar Standards Board
www.barstandardsboard.org.uk
   Statistics:
   www.barstandardsboard.org.uk/media-centre/research-and-
   statistics/statistics/
   www.barstandardsboard.org.uk/media/1585709/bsb_barometer_
   report_112pp_a4_new.pdf

Gray's Inn
www.graysinn.org.uk

The Inner Temple
www.innertemple.org.uk

Lincoln's Inn
www.lincolnsinn.org.uk

The Middle Temple
www.middletemple.org.uk

The Faculty of Advocates in Scotland
www.advocates.org.uk

Northern Ireland Bar
www.barofni.com

Other legal professions

Legal executives
www.cilex.org.uk

Paralegals
www.theiop.org

Licensed conveyancers
www.clc-uk.org

Notaries
www.thenotariessociety.org.uk

Law costs draftsmen
www.associationofcostslawyers.co.uk

Trademark agents
www.itma.org.uk/home

Patent agents
www.cipa.org.uk

Legal secretaries
www.institutelegalsecretaries.com

Legal profession: directories

Chambers UK and Chambers UK Bar Guide
www.chambersandpartners.com

(Chambers publishes comprehensive online directories, containing ranking tables and commentary, of firms of solicitors and barristers' chambers. They are also published annually in print format.)

Legal 500
www.legal500.com
(An in-depth survey of the UK legal profession, also published annually in print format.)

TARGETjobs
https://targetjobs.co.uk/careers-products
(TARGETjobs publishes online graduate careers guides and directories
for various professions including law:
  TARGETjobs: Law
  TARGETjobs: Law vacation schemes & Mini pupillages
  TARGETjobs: Law Pupillages Handbook.)

Law firms gossip
www.rollonfriday.com

Legal systems

Ministry of Justice
www.justice.gov.uk

Wales
www.assemblywales.org

Scotland
www.scotcourts.gov.uk/about-the-scottish-court-service

Northern Ireland
www.niassembly.gov.uk
www.gov.uk/guidance/devolution-settlement-northern-ireland
www.nidirect.gov.uk/index/information-and-services/crime-justice-and-
the-law

Other legal organisations

Crown Prosecution Service
www.cps.gov.uk

Legal Action Group
www.lag.org.uk

Education and training

A levels

Russell Group
www.russellgroup.ac.uk/informed-choices.aspx

UK qualification providers overseas
www.educationuk.org/global/articles/further-education-institutions

Access to Higher Education courses
www.accesstohe.ac.uk

University applications

UCAS
www.ucas.com

> UCAS Parent Guide: Information about the UCAS undergraduate application process
> www.ucas.com/sites/default/files/ucas-parent-guide-2016-entry_0.pdf
> UCAS reference: www.ucas.com/advisers/references/how-write-ucas-undergraduate-references

University guides
www.thecompleteuniversityguide.co.uk
www.theguardian.com/education/ng-interactive/2015/may/25/university-league-tables-2016

LNAT
www.lnat.ac.uk

University of Cambridge law
www.law.cam.ac.uk

University open days
www.opendays.com

Law interviews

Oxford
www.ox.ac.uk/admissions/undergraduate/applying-to-oxford/interviews/interview-timetable?
www.ox.ac.uk/admissions/undergraduate/applying-to-oxford/interviews/sample-interview-questions

Cambridge
www.undergraduate.study.cam.ac.uk/applying/interviews

York
www.york.ac.uk/law/undergraduate/interview/

Fees and funding

UK
www.gov.uk/student-finance

Wales
www.studentfinancewales.co.uk

Scotland
www.saas.gov.uk

Northern Ireland
www.studentfinanceni.co.uk

Overseas students
www.ukcisa.org.uk

Vocational training

GDL course providers
www.sra.org.uk/students/courses/cpe-gdl-course-providers.page

Central Applications Board (for GDL and LPC)
www.lawcabs.ac.uk

Bar Student Application Service (for BPTC)
www.barsas.com

Bar Course Aptitude Test (BCAT)
www.barstandardsboard.org.uk/qualifying-as-a-barrister/bar-profes-sional-training-course/bar-course-aptitude-test

Pupillage Gateway
www.pupillagegateway.com

Funding training

Sponsorship: TARGET jobs
https://targetjobs.co.uk/career-sectors/law-solicitors/305519-which-law-firms-will-fund-your-lpc-and-gdl-course-fees-and-pay-maintenance-costs

Diversity access scheme
www.lawsociety.org.uk/law-careers/diversity-access-scheme/

Career development loans
www.gov.uk/career-development-loans/overview

Careers

www.lawcareers.net
www.simplylawjobs.com

Law reports

www.bailii.org

Useful books

University entrance

Choosing Your Degree Course & University, Brian Heap, Trotman Education, 2014.

HEAP 2017: University Degree Course Offers, Brian Heap, Trotman Education, 2016.

How to Complete Your UCAS Application 2017 Entry, Beryl Dixon, Trotman Education, 2016.

The Times Good University Guide 2016, Times Books, 2015.

Getting into Oxford & Cambridge 2017 Entry, Trotman Education, 2016.

Cut the Cost of Uni, Gwenda Thomas, Trotman, 2012.

LNAT

Practise & Pass Professional: LNAT, Georgina Petrova, Trotman, 2011.

Passing the LNAT, R Hutton and G Hutton, Learning Matters, 2011.

Studying law

Glanville Williams: Learning the Law, A T H Smith, Sweet & Maxwell, 2010.
(This book, first published in 1945, is a very popular introductory book containing lots of useful information on studying law.)

Letters to a Law Student: A Guide to Studying Law at University, Nicholas J McBride, Pearson, 2013.

Learning Legal Rules: A Students' Guide to Legal Method and Reasoning, 8th edition, J A Holland and J S Webb, OUP, 2013.

The English legal system

The English Legal System, Jacqueline Martin, Hodder Education, 2013.

The Law Machine, Marcel Berlins and Clare Dyer, Penguin, 2000.

The Discipline of Law, Lord Denning, OUP, 2005.

The Law (Theory and Practice in British Politics), J Waldron, Routledge, 1990.

Legal Method, Palgrave Macmillan Law Masters, 2013.

Politics of the Judiciary, J A G Griffith, Fontana, 2010.

The criminal justice system and miscarriages of justice

The Juryman's Tale, T Grove, Bloomsbury, 2000.

The Magistrate's Tale, T Grove, Bloomsbury, 2003.

Memoirs of a Radical Lawyer, Michael Mansfield, Bloomsbury, 2010.

Blind Justice: Miscarriages of Justice in Twentieth Century Britain, John Eddleston, ABC-CLIO, 2000.

Standing Accused, M McConville et al, OUP, 1994.

Miscarriages of Justice: A Review of 'Justice in Error', C Walker and K Starmer (eds), OUP, 1999.

A Matter of Justice, M Zander, OUP, 1989.

Careers

Tomorrow's Lawyers: An Introduction To Your Future, Richard Susskind, OUP, 2013.

Is Law for You?: Deciding If You Want to Study Law, Christopher Stoakes, Christopher Stoakes Ltd, 2013.

Professional journals

The Law Society Gazette
www.lawgazette.co.uk
(Publication for solicitors in England and Wales.)

The Lawyer
www.thelawyer.com
(A website for the legal professions containing news, analysis and comment.)

Legal Business
www.legalbusiness.co.uk
(Monthly magazine for legal professionals.)

Legal Action
www.lag.org.uk/magazine
(Monthly magazine of the Legal Action Group, the access to justice charity.)

Glossary

Administrative law
Law governing the duties and operations of the government and public authorities. A branch of public law, usually studied with constitutional law. One of the core subjects.

Advocate
A person who represents someone in court, arguing the case on their behalf. Barristers are the traditional advocates in the English legal system, but solicitors can also now conduct advocacy in certain cases. Advocates in Scotland are the equivalent of English barristers.

Bar
Collective term for the barristers' profession. Aspiring barristers are 'called to the Bar'. The Bar Council is the representative body for barristers.

Bar Professional Training Course (BPTC)
Vocational training course (of one year if studied full-time) for future barristers, taken after completing a law degree (or non-law degree followed by the Graduate Diploma in Law).

Black Letter laws
Well-established laws that are no longer in dispute.

Chambers
Offices occupied by a group of barristers. The term also describes a group of barristers practising from a set of chambers.

Civil law
Can mean either:

- private law, as opposed to criminal, administrative, military and church law; or
- the system of law that grew from Roman law as opposed to the English system of common law.

Common law
Law derived from case law: that is, law created by judges and developed on a case by case basis, rather than laws enacted by Parliament.

Constitutional law
The rules and practices determining how the state is governed, defining the functions of the different entities within a state – i.e. the executive

(government), the legislature (Parliament) and the judiciary, and regulating the relationship between the individual and the state. The constitution of the UK remains largely unwritten, unlike most other states. It is usually studied with administrative law and is one of the core subjects.

Contract law (law of contract)
The law governing contracts, i.e. legally binding agreements (written, verbal or even implied) between two or more parties. Contracts arise as -a result of offer and acceptance, although there are several other criteria that must be satisfied for an agreement to be legally binding. One of the core subjects.

Core subjects
The foundation subjects that must be studied during a degree if the degree is a Qualifying Law Degree, which satisfies the academic stage of training requirements to qualify as a lawyer. Currently these are constitutional and administrative law; contract law; tort; criminal law; equity and trusts; European Union law and property/land law.

Criminal law
The law defining those acts that are deemed to be public wrongs and are therefore punishable by the state in criminal proceedings. Most crimes are made up of two elements – the act itself (*actus reus*) and the thinking behind it (*mens rea*), both of which must be proved 'beyond reasonable doubt' in court to establish guilt. Criminal law is one of the core subjects.

Crown Prosecution Service (CPS)
The CPS, headed by the Director of Public Prosecutions (DPP), is responsible for virtually all the criminal proceedings brought by the police in England and Wales.

Delict (law of delict)
The Scottish name for tort.

Equity
The part of English law originally developed by the Lord Chancellor (and later by the Court of Chancery) to do justice where the common law remedies were limited in scope and flexibility and would lead to an unfair result: equity was more concerned with a fair result than the rigid principles of the law. Even now, equity prevails over the rules of law, but the system of equity is no longer as arbitrary as before. The main areas of equity now cover trusts, property and remedies (e.g. injunctions). 'Anton Piller' orders are a more recent example of equity at work. Equity is studied with trusts as one of the core subjects.

European Union law
The laws of the European Union and how they impact on the English legal system. One of the core subjects.

Evidence
Something that proves the existence or non-existence of a fact. The law of evidence refers to the rules governing the presentation of facts and proof in court, including whether or not evidence is admissible.

Graduate Diploma in Law (GDL)
Also known as the Common Professional Examination (CPE). The one-year (full-time) course that non-law graduates must take to satisfy the academic stage of training to become a lawyer. It covers the seven core subjects that would be studied in a qualifying law degree.

Jurisprudence
The philosophy and theories of law.

Land law (property law)
The law of rights in different types of property and how these rights may be established or transferred. It covers subjects such as mortgages, property trusts, landlord and tenant, leases, easements and covenants. One of the core subjects.

Law school
A law department within a university.

Lay jury
Group of (usually twelve) non-legally qualified people who are selected at random to give a verdict in court.

Legal Practice Course (LPC)
The vocational one-year (full-time) training course taken after graduation with a qualifying degree, or after taking the GDL, and prior to the two-year training contract, designed for intending solicitors.

Moot
A mock courtroom trial of a hypothetical case organised as an extra-curricular/optional activity to help develop legal skills of presenting a clear, logical argument and questioning a witness.

Obligations (law of obligations)
Another name for the laws of tort and contract.

Personal statement
A statement included in the UCAS form setting out why you want to study for your chosen degree at university and why you think you would be a suitable candidate. Arguably the most important part of the UCAS form.

Private law
The parts of the law that deal with the relationships between individuals that are of no direct concern to the state. It includes property law, trusts, contract, tort and family law.

Property law
See land law.

Public law
Law dealing with the constitution and functions of the organs of government, the relationship between individuals and the state and the relationships between individuals that are of direct concern to the state. It includes constitutional law, administrative law, tax law and criminal law.

Pupillage
The final stage of training to become a barrister, involving shadowing a qualified barrister for two six-month periods.

Statute
A law passed by Parliament.

Statute book
All statutes that are currently in force.

Tort
A wrongful act or omission for which the person who has been wronged can obtain damages (i.e. compensation) in a civil court. The definition does not include breaches of contract. Most torts involve personal injury or damage to property caused by negligence. Other torts are defamation, nuisance, etc. The law of tort is one of the core subjects.

Training contract
The two-year period of on-the-job training undertaken by all future solicitors after the LPC in order to complete the vocational stage of training.

Trusts
A legal arrangement whereby one or more trustees hold property for the benefit of one or more beneficiaries. The property is said to be held 'on trust'. Studied with equity as one of the core subjects.